HOSPITALITY AND
AFTER CHRISTENDOM

HOSPITALITY AND COMMUNITY AFTER CHRISTENDOM

Andrew Francis

Paternoster:
thinking faith

This edition first published 2012 by Paternoster
Paternoster is an imprint of Authentic Media Limited
52 Presley Way Crownhill, Milton Keynes, MK8 0ES
www.authenticmedia.co.uk

British Library Cataloguing in Publication Data

A catalogue record for this book is available from the
British Library.

ISBN 978-1-84227-747-8

Cover design by Paul Airy at DesignLeft (www.designleft.co.uk)
Printed and bound in the UK by CPI Group (UK), Croydon, CR4 0YY

Contents

Series Preface

Many Christians have focused on the challenges of post-modernity in recent years, but most have neglected the seismic shifts that have taken place with the disintegration of a nominally Christian society. *After Christendom* is an exciting new series of books exploring the implications of the demise of Christendom and the challenges facing a church now living on the margins of western society.

Post-Christendom, the first volume in the series, investigated the Christendom legacy and raised issues that are further explored in the books that follow. The authors of this series, who write from within the Anabaptist tradition, see the current challenges facing the church not as the loss of a golden age but as opportunities to recover a more biblical and more Christian way of being God's people in God's world. The series addresses a wide range of issues, such as social and political engagement, how we read Scripture, peace and violence, mission, worship, and the shape and ethos of church after Christendom.

These books are not intended to be the last word on the subjects they address, but an invitation to discussion and further exploration. One way to engage in this discussion is via the After Christendom Forum hosted by the Anabaptist Network: www.postchristendom.com

To Mum and Dad – for bringing me up to believe, as well as know, that hospitality and generosity lie at the heart of what daily being a disciple of Jesus means – and in memory of my grandparents' home, where so much of this hospitality began . . .

Acknowledgements

Over nearly thirty years of Christian leadership, I have far too many local congregations and their leaderships to thank each for their welcome. Whether it was just to preach on an occasional Sunday, or as a task-oriented consultant/trainer or as an interim or longer-term minister, all have welcomed me into the circles of their community and enriched that with hospitality, good meals and days of celebration.

But this book owes its genesis to the encouragement of the congregations at Wigton Moor in Leeds, Christ Church in Sevenoaks and Emmanuel Church in Haydon Wick. All these encouraged me to tell 'the story', given that together we have eaten and invited our way through many years of ministry together. But it was my tutors, Peter McEnhill and Dennis Olson, and the JJJ doctoral studies group at Princeton Theological Seminary, New Jersey, USA, who believed that the story's background demanded formal research. Thanks are also due to many friends in the Anabaptist Network who since have encouraged its reworking.

I am grateful to Peter MacDonald, leader of the Iona Community, for his gracious words in the Foreword. Many others gave encouragement too; some provided meals and quiet places in which to write, others read and commented upon pairs of final draft chapters but all are so valued. So thank you to Allan Armstrong ODP, Mark Cawte, Steve Devlin, John Francis, Nicky Green, Janice Heath, Angela Hughes, Alan Kreider, Eleanor Kreider, Sarah Lane Cawte, Noel Moules, Stuart Murray, Annie J. Peters, Pete Rodgers, Jon Smeaton, Jeremy Thomson, Nigel Uden and Philip Walker. It has been my privilege and pleasure to eat with them all, as well as share books and ideas alongside the vibrancy of life and laughter which following Jesus means for us all.

I must also thank the team at Paternoster, particular Mike Parsons as Commissioning Editor, his Readers and the editorial group for their support and willingness to enable this further *After Christendom* publication. Particularly, thank you to Trisha Dale who edited my final text. Their helpful and wise suggestions have enriched this book. I also acknowledge that the mistakes and faults in it are mine.

Foreword

Our world is in turmoil. The Age of Greed has led to a break-down in morality, greater inequality and social crisis. Dictators and oligarchs cling desperately to power and wealth; financial institutions, so engorged they have become too big to fail, have brought the global economy to its knees; and once respected institutions are now tainted by years of compromise, corruption and contagion. The church has not been immune.

Andrew Francis argues that the privileged position enjoyed by the church during the Age of Christendom resulted in the dilu-tion of 'the life-changing and societally challenging message of Jesus' life and ministry'. In Britain today Christians struggle to bring 'good news' to the world as the church becomes increas-ingly marginalized. Yet it is this marginalization which could lead to new life.

Andrew looks to the example of radical streams of Christian discipleship, to movements which against all odds faithfully held to Jesus-shaped patterns of discipleship, to glimpse the emerging shape and practice of the church. We are invited to gather around the table to share food and faith and so recover the prophetic ministry of hospitality through which we glimpse the kingdom of justice and peace.

Andrew's approach is both biographical and scholarly, a com-bination which presents a convincing and hopeful case for the renewal of the church and a more authentic proclamation of the gospel.

Revd Peter Macdonald
Leader
The Iona Community

1

Introduction

Most people in western society enjoy food – particularly if they have the money to choose what they eat and do not suffer from too many health restrictions. That enjoyment is normally increased when the opportunity to eat together with others in a relaxed way presents itself.

Across English-speaking societies and the rest of the world, even the poorest communities mark 'rites of passage' and special occasions by sharing meals.[1] Thinking people do not need sociologists, anthropologists and theologians to delineate that basic fact further as it is essentially and literally a 'gut feeling'.[2]

'The experience of eating so pervades our lives that it practically demands reflection.'[3] But how? As westerners, we occasionally experience shortages of particular foods but never really go hungry. As Christians, we may say grace in a perfunctory manner but are we truly thankful for the costs to our planet and the poor for what is set on our tables? These are big questions, which we ignore for most of the time.

'The act of eating and sharing food is one of the most fundamental gestures of what it means to be human.'[4] Our culture is packed with imagery of eating together, such as Da Vinci's painting, *The Last Supper*, or TV programmes about cooking and dining, just as our high streets are packed with gastropubs, fast-food outlets and coffee houses. The idea of offering hospitality – 'Come for a drink . . . supper . . . dinner' – and the kind of ongoing relationships created, forming transient communities, is everywhere in north-western Europe, including Britain.

'It is important to avoid simply identifying what feels good with being Christian.'[5] This book seeks to make a distinction between finding some lowest common denominator between eating and/or feeling good and/or being Christian. Instead it aims to help each of us develop our thinking, that meals together within everyday Christian lifestyle are important as part of our mission strategy.

This book is the latest volume in the *After Christendom* series, which seeks to examine a number of 'practices' from a radical Christian perspective. If you were unfamiliar with 'post-Christendom' ideas, Stuart Murray's Series Preface provides an important introduction to this concept. At its most basic, Constantine's adoption of Christianity reshaped the nature of sacral culture, moving the church from society's margins to a central position of influence.

This and the other *After Christendom* books show that the life-changing and societally challenging message of Jesus' life and ministry was diluted by that compromising shift. Only the parallel radical streams of Christian discipleship continued to challenge that status quo. As we enter this 'post-Christendom' era these radical streams can help us re-orient vibrant discipleship. Jonathan Bartley, a gifted commentator, political activist and a co-director of the *Ekklesia* Christian think-tank, summarizes this cogently. 'Jesus proclaimed the kingdom in word and deed. He taught the kingdom; he demonstrated the kingdom; he incarnated the kingdom. It is that same kingdom which we are preaching today.'[6]

Even the most cursory survey of the gospels to discover how 'Jesus proclaimed the kingdom in word and deed' brings the searcher to shared meals and eating together. This leads us to the intertwined themes of 'hospitality' and 'community'. Sharing a meal begins with an invitation. When hospitality is given, even if just for a few hours over a meal, a sense of community is fostered. We will explore these ideas later.

In recent Christian Aid weeks, I have been privileged to lead different groups in different ways but using the same threefold theme of 'Gateway – Gathering – Gift'; this has been based on Luke 10:10 and Acts 2:42–7. Both Jesus and the nascent post-Pentecost church recognized that if the faithful were to be gathered, there had to be a gateway into that new community.

Acts 2:42–7 sets out a pattern of gathering with daily meals, expressing both the invitation of Jesus and the growing life of his new community. To gather folks with such numbers and regularity requires forethought – and prayer for active Christians.

In both the biblical testimony and the majority of human experience, 'hospitality involves shared meals; historically table fellowship was an important way of recognizing the equal value and dignity of persons.'[7] If we truly believe, as Jesus' own example demonstrates, that all are made in the 'image of God', no one *may* or can be shunned or turned away, when we develop new patterns of hospitality and community. We can learn from our (grand-) children's desires to be inclusive with invitations to every one of their classmates to their next birthday party.

Whether it is a birthday party, a congregational lunch or a supper with a few intimate friends, good cooks plan their menus. We have to know what ingredients we have got as well as our abilities and skills to use them to their best advantage. Then we must face the 'heat of the kitchen' to ensure that we can bring it all together, that guests are welcomed in such a way that friendships are deepened and we begin to share more of who we really are.

This book is set out in two halves. The four chapters in the first half could be summarized as 'basic ingredients'. Every Christian community knows that without co-ordination its life together falters, and probably will stall if not destroy its missionary purpose – whether that is at the local independent congregational level or as a global denominational policy. The latter is exemplified by the the Roman Catholic Church as it now categorises every country where it has a presence; Britain is now perceived to be a missionary situation. We have to know our story like our store-cupboard, so we know what we have to share with the world.

- The first chapter helps us revisit the biblical traditions in the Hebrew Scriptures (Old Testament), which tumble across into the New Testament.
- The second chapter asks what we can learn from the experiences of the radical tradition, before, during and after Christendom.
- For most Christians, Holy Communion or the Lord's Supper is central and key to the nature and understanding of faith. But how we celebrate and share that declares the nature of the church's hospitality and community, which is the subject of the third chapter.

- This naturally questions how our hospitality determines the shape of the local church, the nature of our community and its theology. The fourth chapter asks: How does your story and my story shape practice?

The four chapters in the second half examine the 'heat of the kitchen'. At some point we must move on from the already-learned to take risks if we are to develop. As I learned to cook in a busy professional kitchen, there came a moment when the chef said, 'Step up to the piano', meaning 'Stand at the main oven and oversee production'. The even tougher moment was at 'the Pass', where the chef examined each plateful to ensure it was worthy before the waiters served it up to the waiting customer. As Christians, if we are serious about 'hospitality' and 'community', we must accept the heat of the kitchen.

- How do we build the new 'community of the kingdom'? Chapter 6 offers three models of 'developing patterns' of shared meals and congregational hospitality.
- If we are to create a 'gateway', it must be open to where people are and begin to meet their needs. In Chapter 7 we explore some kinds of Christian community for those opting into 24/7 discipleship in a secular post-Christendom world.
- Chapter 8 explores: What kind of leadership is necessary if we are to find the key to Jesus-shaped vision and appropriate strategy?
- Chapter 9 considers the building-blocks necessary to facilitate the growth of a Christian community from 'just a Sunday congregation'. In facing post-Christendom, inherited churches will need to find their way to transition.

Finally, there is a short concluding section:

- A set of five conclusions.
- Two table liturgies: one for congregational usage and another for home use.
- A select bibliography – of cookbooks, practical theology and helpful works on hospitality and community.

Now that you have read the menu, let me invite you to dine . . .

Part 1

Hospitality and Community: Some Ingredients

2

What Does the Bible Say?

I grew up within an Anabaptist-oriented[1] conference of churches. For them, it was the story, ministry and example of Jesus that were given most attention. It was natural to be excited about the radical difference of Jesus, and all that he stood for, and to model both our lives and how we lived together according to Jesus' words and ways.

However, apart from the Jesus stories, that is the gospels, one New Testament narrative continually hit me like an electric shock. This was Luke's account of the example and lifestyle of the church shortly after Pentecost in Acts 2:42–7. There the believers met daily together, not only praying and learning about Jesus, but eating together and sharing all that they had. This reminded me of the network of congregations in which I grew up in Scotland, then Manchester and, later, in Birmingham.

The twin themes of 'hospitality' and 'community' did not even need thinking about or identifying. This is what the Jesus community did – then and now. The Bible confirmed this. As a teenager, I went to grammar school with Jewish friends who occasionally invited me to their homes to join in their Friday Passover meal. Every time they used the Hebrew words which declared 'My father was a wandering Aramean' (Deut. 26:5) they reminded themselves that God had provided for them every step of the way. With them, I discovered how 'our' Jesus practice (as Christians) was rooted within the Friday evening meal of Jewish tradition.

Old Testament – the Hebrew Witness

At the very heart of the creation narratives, God's provision is affirmed: 'God saw all that he had made, and it was very good' (Gen. 1:31). This provision included food: 'I have provided all kinds of grain and all kinds of fruit for you to eat' (Gen. 1:29, GNB). Humanity was accorded stewardship of earth's resources, including food.

Two key 'Law Book'[2] judgement passages involve discernment over food.

- Adam and Eve are warned not to 'eat from the tree of the knowledge of good and evil' (Gen. 2:17), on pain of death. The Fall is rooted in not simply human disobedience but also in the lack of recognition of what may be shared. 'Inasmuch as food normally sustains life, the choice of this particular restriction as a test of human obedience proves understandable.'[3]
- In patriarchal history, in Jacob's duplicity in tricking his dying father, while supplying his favourite food, to help gain Isaac's final blessing (Gen. 27), Jacob used food to entice his brother Esau to give up his birthright as the eldest son (Gen. 25:29–34); again food is instrumental to this part of faith's history.

But this culminates in the Deuteronomic tradition which centres upon revealing a God who 'defends the cause of the fatherless and the widow, and loves the alien, giving him food and clothing' (Deut. 10:18). The nature of a community is revealed in the pattern of its hospitality towards those who cannot demand it. Further in the deliverance narratives found in Exodus, the motif of food is vital.

- The very promise of God is to lead his people to 'a land flowing with milk and honey' (Exod. 3:8); the promise is for a land of abundance, including that of food, which can be shared within the community of faith.
- At the heart of that Hebrew 'deliverance' understanding is the Passover (Exod. 12). The gathering of the extended family to share a meal in particular ways not only has an ongoing significance but also identifies them as part of that community of

faith. It is vital for this study to note that Deuteronomy 16:11 affirms that resident aliens share in the Passover, alongside Israelites as part of that community of faith's extended family, just as my Jewish friends invited this Gentile to Friday-evening supper.

- During that forty years' sojourn in the wilderness, in days of need the Israelites were sustained by the daily gift of manna (Exod. 16:35), and later by quail and water (Exod. 16 – 17). That celebrated provision of God (Exod. 16:4; Ps. 78:23ff.) continued until their deliverance was complete (Josh. 5:12) when they entered the Promised Land. That miraculous provision continued more specifically in the days of the prophets; Elijah's ministry was sustained by ravens and a meal within a widow's household (1 Kgs 17).

During the period of the 'monarchy', meals continued to hold significance for Israel:

- Different models of hospitality are revealed in Judges 14:10ff.; 19; Ruth 2:14ff. These are rooted in the desert tradition (e.g. Gen. 19; 43; Exod. 2:20ff.), which provides both sustenance and shelter (i.e. protection) for the guest, be they friend or stranger.
- Such 'openness' contrasts with the 'closed' nature of sacrificial meals used to celebrate the commissioning of individuals, such as Gideon (Judg. 6:19ff.) and Saul (1 Sam. 9:12ff.).

But it was not just in the tradition of the Law, but also that of the Prophets that God's rich provision is celebrated:

- God's provision was active, as stated above in the Elijah (1 Kgs 17) example or in miracle working, such as Elisha's in 2 Kings 4.
- Equally vital, we should note the breadth of prophetic utterances which affirmed that God's promise would ultimately reign. One of the strongest examples is from Isaiah: 'On this mountain the LORD of hosts will make for all peoples a feast of rich food, a feast of well-matured wines' (25:6, NRSV) – a declaration of the eschatological banquet. This affirmed for Israel that the God who has acted will bring all things to his purpose, providing for all people.

- It is in Isaiah 55:1–2 that the key to God's invitation is declared: 'You who have no money, come, buy . . . buy . . . without money and without cost.' God's hospitality is not dependent upon humanity except in the positive response which individuals need to make to receive divine provision.

In this study, it is important to recognize the breadth of purpose in the experience of shared meals within the Hebrew tradition. Brevity precludes comprehensive study. Omissions must be acknowledged; for example, the fellowship meal offerings in Leviticus which, on later occasions, included invitations to the poor.

Yet on each occasion, how food is shared (or not) tells us something about the community which began as a bunch of 'wandering Arameans'. Because of this experience they came together as a tribal confederation, discovering that the Lord was moulding them as 'the people of God' – the community of God's people.

In recognition of that, the Hebrew tribes gathered in worship, expressing both lament and praise. This contrast is most notably found in the book of Psalms. Brevity prevailing, we need to turn to only two of the most popularly used psalms to recognize the hand of God's provision in the making of their 'community' and the exercise of its 'hospitality':

- Psalm 121 opens with a call to recognize the Creator God in the world around us and closes with the affirmation that this same God will safeguard all our comings and goings.
- More explicitly, Psalm 23 tells how God prepares 'a table before me' – a very personal assurance.

Gospels

The four canonical gospels record twenty-eight instances of meals. Even if the parallel passages within Matthew, Mark and Luke are deducted, this still leaves *at least* seventeen significant occasions on which a meal is central to that piece of ministry of Jesus and his disciples.

The parables of salt (Matt. 5:13ff.), the yeast (Matt. 13:33), the needs of a late-night visitor (Luke 11:5ff.) and new wine (Matt. 9:17ff.) demonstrate Jesus' illustrative use of everyday commodities. The miracles at the Cana wedding (John 2) and the feeding of the five thousand (Matt. 14:13ff.) demonstrate Jesus' use of what is available for particular meals to reveal the kingdom of God more fully. In these snapshot episodes, it is easy to pick out the themes of hospitality and community.

Jesus invites his followers to 'Seek his kingdom, and these things will be given to you as well' (Luke 12:31). What kind of assumption underpins Jesus' meaning for these words? Is it that to participate in the kingdom will mean sharing in the provision of God's good earth? Must that include food, if the kingdom is to provide some measure of physical well-being? The Jesus of the so-called Synoptic Gospels[4] is revealed as one who confronts any kind of social exclusivity because this contradicts his kingdom teaching.[5]

Academic scholarship generally accepts that the gospel writers' economy of words means that what is included has particular significance. 'The attention given in the Gospels to meals is well known. As a primary context for understanding Jesus, his meals are an embodiment of his acceptance of outcasts and a demonstration of the grace and presence of the kingdom.'[6] The assurance of God's provision, and the very human petition for 'daily bread' in the Lord's Prayer (Matt. 6:5ff.; Luke 11:1ff.) both form part of that demonstration of the kingdom; 'the promise of the next meal was also an assurance of the kingdom'.[7]

Whatever commentators, or any readers, make of the account of the feeding of the five thousand, it is the only miracle to be recorded in all four gospels.[8] This increases the potential not only for its actual veracity but also for its fundamental significance. For this study, it is what it demonstrates that is important. Jesus utilizes what is seemingly a ridiculously small amount of food and yet a multitude are fed. This is not to argue that Christian miracles occur in every context of Christian gathering but that Jesus models that 'communities of faith' must be open to sharing all that they have, however little, to reveal God's abundance. Whether a group is a community (or not) can perhaps be more easily determined by its use of resources in times of hardship and little, than it can in days of peace and plenty.

In one of the judgement parables, Jesus commends those who provided for him: 'for I was hungry and you gave me something to eat, I was thirsty and you gave me something to drink' (Matt. 25:35ff.). It is important to note that the sharing of resources (or the failure to share resources) will be, in Jesus' own words, one of the factors upon which humanity will be judged. Christian hospitality is not just about how we invite our best friends to supper (Matt. 5:47) but also the 'stranger in our midst' to Sunday lunch.

In the exercise of his ministry, Jesus followed the pattern of travelling Jewish teachers.[9] Koenig identifies a key paradox of the radicalism of Jesus' ministry: 'while Jesus and the Twelve had given up possessions and regular family life, they nevertheless manifested abundance, especially at meals, and invited others to share in it.'[10] Rightly, Schüssler Fiorenza is one of the key advocates that women were part of Jesus' wider travelling circle. So, in this group, teaching and meals would be a natural and normal context in which the sexes could mix,[11] in contrast to wider Jewish society in Jesus' days. The hospitality of Martha and Mary's Bethany home (John 11 – 12) demonstrates this.

Yet Jesus' ministry remains counter-cultural, in breaking other barriers than the mixing of men and women. 'Most writers now agree that "eating with sinners" was one of the most characteristic and striking marks of Jesus.'[12] The inclusion of Levi into the Twelve (Mark 2:13ff.) or the affirmation of Zacchaeus (Luke 19:1ff.) reveals that such behaviour was normal for Jesus, whether in the ongoing daily relationship with Levi, as part of the Twelve, or the (seemingly) one-off encounter with Zacchaeus.

Food, and its sharing, seems central to Jesus' own ways and his revealing of the kingdom of God, in word, deed and prayer. If being a disciple is to follow the way of Jesus, there is a significant Jesus pattern of sharing food, across the boundaries of society. This counter-cultural practice of Jesus, shown in the gospels, means that it has much to say to the Christian church today. Now that shifting economic patterns of society create greater marginalization, churches need to echo Jesus' practice in their hospitality.

Meals in the New Testament 'After' the Gospels

In contrast to the gospel writers, apart from three references in Acts (2:42ff.; 6:1-4; 20:7ff.), one in 2 Peter (2:13) and one in Jude (v. 12), the only New Testament references to actual 'common meals' or 'eating together' are from Paul, the evangelist and church-planter. The question this raises is whether the frequency and practice of shared meals was so common that it did not merit extra attention in the correspondence between New Testament communities, or was it so infrequent that only the abuses were dealt with. This question remains unresolved between academic commentators.

On balance, the non-Pauline references (itemized above) imply a regularity of practice whether in the burgeoning Jerusalem and Troas contexts or in the Peter-founded congregations, where infiltrators abused the local practice. In Acts 2:42ff., 'The much discussed question whether the "breaking of bread" here refers to the Eucharist or to another common meal does not much matter here. In any case, it is a specific activity tied to the person of Jesus, which then continues unchanged after Pentecost.'[13] Lindemann, following this argument, goes on to explain that '"the breaking of bread" is not meant as a cultic action, but the common mealtime held in houses'.[14]

The concept of regular common meals, within the Christian community, is substantiated by the recognition of supportive passages. The writer to the Hebrews had to make this practice of hospitality explicit, 'Do not forget to entertain strangers, for by so doing some people have entertained angels without knowing it' (Heb. 13:2). Was this because they were ignoring a practice that was deemed both necessary and vital to New Testament-era Christians?

Within the developing New Testament church, the nature of Christian fellowship involves eating together: 'Here I am! I stand at the door and knock. If anyone hears my voice and opens the door, I will come in and eat with him, and he with me' (Rev. 3:20). If Revelation's writer is not simply a divine amanuensis, his vision of Jesus' response to the earthly believer will have been shaped, in part, by his experience of the practice of the Christian community he was part of or been part of before exile. Some assume the lack of direct reference support this case: 'given the paucity of other forms of table fellowship in Acts through Revelation . . . it appears relatively straightforward to argue that Jesus' table fellowship with sinners remained quite distinctive.'[15]

Pauline scholars differ on the nature of how Jesus' table fellowship remained quite distinctive. The issue here has two aspects. One is the question of whether every common meal included celebration (in words and form) of the Lord's Supper; that is an unanswerable question because of our lack of data. The second is whether the nature of the Lord's Supper, when set within common meals, is cultic, which would make the practice of 'common meals' a cultic phenomenon.

To offer two poles of thought: Meeks's view is that 'in the Pauline, and even the pre-Pauline tradition, the celebration is understood as a cultic commemoration of Jesus'.[16] By contrast, Banks states: 'Sharing a meal in the Lord's Name was a Christian practice before Paul's churches appeared on the scene . . . One would most naturally expect the Lord's Supper to be part of what took place . . . Nowhere does Paul suggest that the Lord's Supper has any cultic significance.'[17]

What is without doubt in the New Testament canon is that patterns of fellowship (Gk: *koinonia*) were a mark of these newly forming Christian communities. Leaders, their envoys and associates received hospitality as they travelled.

Koenig develops the idea that '*philoxein*, the term for hospitality in the New Testament refers literally not to a love of strangers but to a delight in the whole guest-host relationship, in the mysterious reversals and gains for all parties which take place'.[18] The logical extrapolation of this *philoxein* usage rather than *xenizein* (Gk: to receive a guest) is that in the sharing of hospitality – that is the sharing of food, as against the simple generosity of provision – there is an intrinsic transaction of grace. For me, the New Testament supports the practice of common meals as part of sharing fellowship and offering hospitality.

The Last Supper

Upon critical examination, there are few narratives which appear in all four gospels (e.g. the calling of disciples, the feeding of the five thousand, the Passion and Resurrection). A key passage, which does, is that of the Last Supper (Matt. 26:26–30; Mark 14:22–6; Luke 22:14–23; John 13 – 14). For the purpose of this study, it is important to note that it is only the Synoptic Gospels which make this meal eucharistic in the sense of Jesus' instruction to partake of bread and wine (in whichever order).

The vital thing, which all the gospel writers record, is that on the eve of Passover, therefore the evening of Jesus' arrest, the disciples shared a meal with Jesus. Sharing a meal was not questioned by the disciples; it was simply the 'Jesus way' of being together. It is this latter fact which becomes important as we think afresh about themes of 'hospitality' and 'community'.

The 'End Times'

The banquets in Esther 8 – 9 help to establish a background for the concept of the eschatological[19] banquet; reference has already been made to Isaiah 25:6ff. The way that a feast is celebrated can tell of the future hope of that community. The book of Psalms contains contrasting images of being sustained in the face of adversity (Ps. 23) or sharing in God's abundance (Ps. 36); both reflect that the shared table is a sign of the 'age to come'.

Donahue has argued that there is a three-level significance between the meals of the earthly Jesus, the eucharistic community and the eschatological banquet.

> Meals in Jesus' fellowship became practical parables as evocative as his verbal parables . . . each meal was a proleptic celebration of God's Kingdom. Jeremias in his study of the Lord's Prayer provides clear evidence that in its original, and shorter, Aramaic form, the Lord's Prayer links the petition for bread and the final coming of the Kingdom. Celebrating the latter as the messianic banquet, gives greater strength to Jeremias' argument that 'daily bread' should truly be translated as the 'bread of the Coming Day'.[20]

Yet the Lord's command is to pray that for *this* day and not just tomorrow.

Following Schweitzer's foundational work on New Testament eschatology,[21] twentieth-century biblical scholarship ranged across different understandings of the end times or 'eschaton'. What could be agreed was that these concepts ranged around different interpretations of the two central closing concepts of the canon: one was 'the great supper of God' (Rev. 19:17) and the other was the 'Second Coming of Christ in glory'.[22] As Wainwright summarizes, 'the eucharist is already a meal, and the Bible's favourite picture for the final kingdom is that of feasting.'[23]

In Chapter 4, 'Gathering at the Table', we will return to the question of both what we are celebrating and what we are looking forward to, as the community gathers to share bread and wine, in the name of Jesus.

Concluding Remarks

A credible reading of the Christian Bible demonstrates that the appropriate use of food, in a variety of shared meals, is central to its narrative. In moving from the provision of God's abundance, through the ministry of Jesus and his followers in the New Testament church to the final banquet, the motif of the shared meal is, at least, beneficial for understanding the journey of the 'community of faith'.

It is hardly surprising that in a predominantly nomadic culture, as was the nature of the tribal confederation in Israel's history, the hospitality of a shared meal is important. Equally, to have not regarded times of feasting and celebration as occasions to celebrate the blessing of God would have been strange. Thus the biblical narrative almost logically has to point toward hospitality and sharing food as expressions of God's blessing. In turn, that welcome and hospitality declared something about the nature of God's community of believers.

3

Radical Streams

Almost weekly, my grammar-school headmaster admonished me and my crowd of friends, saying, 'If it's counter-cultural or rebellious, you support it.' That grain of truth has grown, in my case, into a faith and political philosophy, which questions any 'might is right' society.

Nowhere was this more apparent as I grew up then in that radical, believers'-baptism movement. I was a 'preacher's kid' whose dad talked a different language from that of local vicars and Catholic priests. Our congregations had to earn their street-corner buildings and the right to be heard. At primary school, when a visiting Anglican vicar asked who went to church, my hand shot up. As my turn came to answer, he told me that mine was 'not a proper church'.

So what was the 'proper church' in early 1960s Britain?

All I knew is that we did what Jesus asked. Poor people were given our spare clothes and extra blankets. We fed the homeless at the door. We went to worship where anyone, including me, could get up and pray for those in need by name. Our church went camping, taking urban estate kids who had never been away or seen a cow or the sea.

So we baptized those who could tell their own life-changing story of encountering Jesus. Unlike my school-friends, we did not go to christenings where water was thrown over unsuspecting babies, who could not understand what was happening. My dad preached about Jesus, not someone whom others called 'Christ'. You remember these things as a child.

Christendom

Although I did not know it as an 8 year old, I had encountered the Christendom mentality, in that vicar's response. (Readers of previous volumes in this *After Christendom* series[1] may wish to skip the next five paragraphs.)

At its most basic, Christendom was that part of the western world in which there was both a complicit and explicit relationship between church and state. This ensured that Christianity was the prescribed religion of those constituent countries. At various times, all other faiths were either proscribed or treated as the heathen enemy. An example of the latter would be the Muslim occupiers of Jerusalem at the time of the twelfth-century crusades. At other points, within the Christendom nations, Dissenters from the state-sanctioned churches were persecuted, exiled, forced to recant and sometimes executed.

Within the life of the Christendom church, the hierarchical model of bishop-priest-deacon was preferred over other egalitarian New Testament patterns of ministry (such as in Eph. 5). By the time of its split from the Orthodox Communion in 1054, the western Roman Catholic Church's leaders were powerful men, commanding wealth and resources. Perhaps it is little surprise that they emulated the patterns of the Roman Empire in utilizing the costly Tyrian purple for episcopal robes. The church was declaring its pope and bishops to hold the kind of power previously only accorded the emperor and his generals.

If a church is to have such leadership, then logically there must be the foot-soldiers, the followers or those to be 'led'. To keep order, there had to be both conformity and uniformity. One practical outworking of this was the adoption of the Latin Mass as the ubiquitous act of public worship. Another was coherence to the state-sanctioned practices of religion, such as infant baptism or acceptance of the Creed. Dissent could not be tolerated and punishment was extreme. All this cost money, so one mark of the Christendom church was the reintroduction of the Old Testament practice of 'tithing' – giving the first 10 per cent of one's goods and income to the church.

This meant that by the Middle Ages, Christendom was the new western European empire. The Roman Catholic Church had more wealth than many of its constituent countries, utilizing its power to enable vassal kings to rule regionally and locally. All this is a far cry from the Galilean Jesus of the gospels, who sided with the poor and outcast against the religious hierarchy of his day.

It set a trend, confirmed by the twentieth-century church, as it supported wars, oppression and inquisition, further becoming an instrument of the state. This enabled the church's leaders and its voice to be heard 'centre stage' within our society. Once I went with a childhood friend to Sunday school where we sang 'the rich man in his castle, the poor man at his gate, all things high and lowly, God gives them their estate' – a verse expunged from my home congregation's hymnbooks. In that popular hymn, Christendom was declared and the Jesus I knew had been squeezed out.

Before Christendom

However, many centuries before, Constantine made choices which have affected the nature of western Europe and the world until the present day. Before those imperial choices, Christianity was neither uniform nor conformist. Brevity demands that only a few snapshots can be shared.

Returning briefly to the New Testament era, clearly the lifestyle of the early Christians was sufficiently counter-cultural in Acts 2:42–7 and the later passages in Acts and Paul, referring to the sharing of homes, wealth and goods, to merit specific mention. Banks's helpful but speculative *Going to Church in the First Century*[2] highlights the egalitarian nature ('neither Jew nor Greek, slave nor free' – Gal. 3:28) as it gathered to eat, worship, pray and learn together. Indeed when this common practice was abused or excesses crept in, apostles like Paul took enough trouble to write their rebuke (1 Cor. 11:33ff.). Hospitality and welcome were at the heart of the Christian community whether it gathered centrally each day or met in shared houses.

The neon phrase of Wayne A. Meeks, the New Testament commentator: *'the resocialization into an alternative community'*[3] animates both my own and other contemporary Anabaptist-Mennonite educators' teaching and writing[4] as it summarizes the Christian way of being in welcome and community.

But it was not all sweetness and easy travelling. Acts reveals this in chapter 11 as Peter meets Cornelius the Gentile centurion, eating with him before reporting back to a far more orthodox, Jewish-oriented Jerusalem church. Despite their reservations, the Jerusalem Christians learnt new perspectives about God's new community in the sharing of gifts with their sisters and brothers in Macedonia.

Yet within a century or so, non-Christian sources[5] speak of the way Christians met – often by night and behind closed doors, in private homes. By AD 70, churches did not allow non-believers to attend worship. Therefore it must have been the lifestyle, hospitality and sense of community which drew people to accept Jesus as Lord. The *Apostolic Tradition of Hippolytus*[6] describes in detail a highly organized rite of believers' baptism, requiring many weeks of preparation, including the new converts living together in community for the weeks beforehand.

Church history documents the importance of the Desert Fathers. These were early Christian theologians who lived in the wilderness in some types of extended community, possibly only meeting for worship and meals together on a Sunday, spending the rest of the week in solitude. Such communities formed the foundation for later monasticism.

The early medieval rise of institutional monasticism, with its professed orders of nuns and/or monks, enforced celibacy and several mandatory daily services, marked a highly committed pattern of Christian discipleship. During the post-Constantinian era, 'as proved by Augustine . . . and many others, it was quite possible for bishops (and others) to perform their administrative, pastoral and liturgical functions while living in a monastic household'.[7] Orthodox in belief but communitarian in lifestyle, these Christian leaders lived a very different life from the local populace. Sadly, as a professor of medieval history has discovered, food was used as an instrument of discipline.[8]

Some Radical Alternatives to Christendom Ways

Once Christendom was establishing, the church's need to be an alternative society diminished almost by inverse proportion.

If everyone in Christian society is deemed to be a Christian (sometimes with mandatory baptism for infants), the need to demonstrate that one is a Christian has gone. If you are expected to be *automatically* a believer and therefore an attendee at Christian worship, at least on high days and holy days, you do not need to gather for other specifically Christian occasions. As Alan Kreider has logically argued, the need for mission is also lost if and when a Christendom society decides everyone within it is Christian.[9]

The further natural, logical observation is that this will lead to lowest-common-denominator Christianity. For those who believe discipleship demands particular ethical stances, whether:

- adopting non-violence,
- giving more than a tithe (church taxes),[10]
- solely Sunday observance of faith.

Christendom is reductionist. Over the Christendom centuries, a whole variety of Christian groups accepted these radical values as part of a more defined pattern of Christian discipleship. In each of the following paragraphs, the beliefs and practice of some of these radically different alternative (to the Christendom mainstream) groups are highlighted.

Within Britain until the late Middle Ages, the vast majority of permanent places of worship were either part of abbeys or monasteries or on manorial estates.[11] All were places of protection, welcome and hospitality and, therefore, of food. Logic implies that if the populace travelled some distance to corporate worship, the sharing of food would be a natural part of both the journey and the gathering of the faithful: consider Chaucer's *Canterbury Tales*. Bede records the Northumbrian king, Oswald, feeding the faithful as they gathered for worship.[12]

. . . and all across Europe

Saxby explains the European 'rise of separating nonconformists'[13] (such as Asia Minor's Paulicians or Hungary's Bogomils) by the late Middle Ages, recognizing that 'mutual aid . . . was characteristic of them' in the sharing of food, clothing and shelter. Because of their extreme persecution, few records now exist to detail this. However, the Beguines in the Low Countries,[14] Cathars in France,[15] Waldensians in Italy, northern Europe's Brethren of the Common Life[16] and Anabaptists[17] demonstrate that successive waves of separatist but communitarian, radical Christianity, all across Europe, were part of the reaction to mainstream, institutional Christendom. Focusing on the most prevalent of these extant groups is useful.

Academic ambiguity continues on whether the Waldensian movement of the late Middle Ages drew their name from their founder Peter Waldo or the Italian alpine Waldensian valleys in which they made their home. They shared many values, such as simplicity or community of goods or commitments to equality with the almost contemporary Franciscan movement. Waldensians were treated as heretical by the Roman Catholic Church, so exiled themselves for safety. In the Alps, some lived communally, others in family clusters but all practised hospitality towards friend and stranger. Today in their congregations and centres in both Europe and the Americas, Waldensians regularly share meals as part of their common life, attesting to their practices of hospitality and community.[18]

Stories abound of St Francis of Assisi, about his 'call to simplicity' and a life of peace-making, the rejection of worldly wealth and the sharing of earthly goods. Francis' itinerant preaching ministry, and those of his followers, unlike Waldo's, was not rejected by the Roman Church. In turn this led to a first Order of travelling friars, a second Order of nuns, known as the Poor Clares, and more recently a third Order of professed lay Franciscans. The sharing of food and shelter, as well as a call to radical community, rooted in a vibrant Jesus-oriented spirituality still marks out tenty-first-century Franciscans.[19]

Early in the sixteenth century, three disparate and unrelated groups, in the northern Netherlands, the Zurich canton and south Germany, shared meals and New Testament study. All became convicted that church and state must be separate and the congregations should be comprised of only adult believers. This led them to be baptized as believers, enabling their enemies to call them re-baptizers or Anabaptists. Despite terrible persecution, the movement grew and spread. Some fled to Eastern Europe, becoming communitarian, resurfacing later as the

Bruderhof. The Friesland supporters of Menno Simons became known as Mennonites – in turn nurturing the first English Baptist leaders. Also, Mennonites spawned another self-exiling group who lived in family clusters, becoming known as the Amish. Shared meals, hospitality and some form of intimate community help define the wider Anabaptist movement today.[20]

The first English Independents (later called Congregational-ists) were gatherings of radical Christians into lay- (rather than clergy-) led congregations. They were also often forced to meet in barns or the open air. In an attempt at suppression of such radi-cals, the 1665 Five Mile Act effectively stopped Dissenting minis-ters from preaching less than five miles from their previous churches.[21] So they and their followers often trekked several miles to worship together. There are English county records document-ing such meeting – and eating – together. One of my favourite places in England is the Avebury stone circle. At its heart is an early (1660s) Nonconformist chapel where folks gathered safely to eat and worship, listening to Dissenting preachers; the sur-rounding market towns of Devizes, Marlborough and Calne are each just over five miles away.

Burgeoning movements often relied on the hospitality of wealthy supporters. Thus, George Fox and other itinerant preachers travelled the country bringing together a movement, commonly known as the Quakers. Records show that people were gathered with song to hear Fox and others preach sermons punctuated by shared meals, either in local homes or on the hill-sides. Quaker histories record how local groups lived in separate households but in close community, exercising mutual hospita-lity and care for their neighbours.[22] Later Quaker industrialists such as the Cadburys in Bourneville and the Frys in York devel-oped garden suburbs, with allotments, for their workers. Each home's garden had an apple and a pear tree, instead of the bibli-cally enjoined 'vine and fig-tree' (Mic. 4:4), as another sign of God's blessing. Today, I rarely attend a Quaker meeting as a vis-itor without a member offering me a meal invitation.

In the nineteenth-century coming together of various small bands of Christians, each understood that the New Testament way of discipleship was not to be found in the established churches. Groups like the Campbellites, the Darbyites and Scotch

Baptists were essentially congregational in polity and Anabaptist in theology. Members had to be baptized as professing believers to share in weekly lay- (not clergy-) led Communion services. Two distinct strands emerged: the Churches of Christ and the (Plymouth) Brethren. Anabaptist in style but avowedly committed to 'restore' the New Testament order, they became known as Restorationists.[23] Their local congregations grew, as workmates shared meals, 'gossiping the gospel', and their regional gatherings were marked by the sharing of food, worship and teaching. I grew up in this tradition.

While this 'radical alternatives' section can never be comprehensive, it provides historic snapshots which still have enough repercussions today to encourage interim conclusions (while recognizing this writer's selectivity!). Their use of meals stands in sharp contrast to the lack of meals' documentation in the practice of the Methodist 'class meeting'. While some Anglican friends will say that their harvest supper or Easter-morning breakfast has been happening since pussy was a cat, their experience is not typical across the whole Anglican tradition. Some such examples are obviously only annual events.

Within the radical tradition, the practice of eating together, shared meals, hospitality and a real sense of community (through shared lives if not homes) is part of the fabric of discipleship. These historic snapshots continue into this generation.

After Christendom

Each volume in this *After Christendom* series has to wrestle with the difficult concept of how, when and where Christendom is ending. This task is like nailing jelly to the wall. It can never have a date like the Battle of Hastings or even be identified like the 'you never had it so good' era of the 1960s.

Instead, there has been a gradual erosion of the church's influence in western society and while church-state links may be retained, no longer does the church or Christian teaching retain significant influence in the lives of 95 per cent of the UK population. The church has been pushed from centre stage to the margins, or even out of sight for that majority.

The trend is similar across Europe. In 1912, France severed church-state links and although the country is littered with crucifixes, Catholicism is increasingly vestigial. In northern Europe, most Lutheran Christians in Scandinavia and Germany have increasingly supported the severance of church-state links.

In Britain, only the Welsh have accepted disestablishment in the episcopal Church of Wales. The Presbyterian Church of Scotland, despite their membership crises, *may* have claim to remain established, because of their greater reach and influence across Scotland, as well as no political interference in the selection of senior leaders. The Anglican Church of England in many areas means little or nothing to the majority of local populace – yet the Prime Minister recommends to the Queen which priests should become bishops.

... and against the tide

However against this, there are significant signs of hope from Christianity at the margins. Intriguingly, two such influential examples began as initiatives of Reformed Church pastors around the time of the Second World War.

The story of how a shy Swiss pastor, Roger Schutz, lived out his academic research with a group of postgraduates in a proto-community is often told.[24] Moving to poverty-stricken Taizé, sheltering refugees from the Nazis, the eponymous community grew around its practice of thrice-daily prayer and thrice-daily shared meals. Now, every summer, tens of thousands of predominantly young people flock to share this life. They examine daily Jesus' call to simplicity and peace-making in seminars led by a Taizé brother. Despite the community's desire not to spawn a denomination, many large UK cities host both Taizé-style congregations and, more importantly, informal neighbourhood Taizé 'cells', which frequently meet for food and prayer as radical discipleship groups.

Almost simultaneously with Taizé, a Church of Scotland minister, George MacLeod, a brilliant preacher, decorated war-hero-turned-pacifist and leader of people, became sickened by the poverty, unemployment and waste of urban Glasgow. Taking a group of trainee ministers and unemployed craftsmen, George led them to Iona where they rebuilt the ruined abbey. Daily they shared work, food and prayer, making this the model for the present Iona Community – made up of lay and ordained Christians. Hospitality and eating together became a mark of this now world-famous and growing community. Local Iona groups meet monthly across the world for food, prayer and mutual encouragement. The community is just re-introducing neighbourhood Columban houses, where four or five activist supporters will live together, offering hospitality and community ministry.[25]

In a much lesser way in the UK, the pattern of the autonomous Catholic Worker Movement houses echoes the work of Iona's Columban houses. Inspired by the work of Dorothy Day,[26] a ministry of hospitality and community, enhanced by the sharing of daily meals with whoever was there, told of Jesus' welcome in 'eating with tax-gatherers and sinners' far more than the might and power of the Roman Catholic Church. I first encountered a Birmingham Catholic Worker household as a teenager, thanks to the underground Christian magazine, *Catonsville Roadrunner*. That household ensured my ongoing involvement with the Birmingham Peace Centre, further radicalizing my faith, as I experienced theirs and others' hospitality changing lives.

At the same time, some of my churchgoing friends lost patience with the traditionalism of their parents' congregations, joining things called 'House Churches'. Some were exciting communities which I encountered as part of a film crew, filming the travelling Jesus-People evangelist, Arthur Blessitt. He told us of shared Christian households on Sunset Strip, which inspired some of that crew to begin a similarly styled household in Birmingham.

Breaking the mould?

But most House Churches met in someone's front room, singing to the accompaniment of guitars or keyboards, sharing coffee and, unsurprisingly to my radical Christianity, an expected willingness to share their faith. House churches grew phenomenally, forging alliances, developing trans-national ministries and evolved into what is now known as the New Church Movement.[27] Although a few dabbled with shared households, none adopted this consistently; but what is remarkable is how little they developed any pattern of shared meals or common hospitality evangelistically. But they are a clear sign that one major part of Britain's Christian growth is rejecting the denominations and churchmanship of the Christendom era.

In stunning contrast, the vision of a small Baptist church in rural Northamptonshire for shared New Testament-styled households led to the formation of the Anabaptist-oriented Jesus Fellowship, with its militant evangelical Jesus Army. Their 'common purse' communities, ranging from a country mansion to inner-city households, are the norm for all committed members. Visitors are welcomed to stay, eat and work alongside them. Hospitality and community are at the heart of this burgeoning community with around thirty households, several urban church centres, evangelistic teams, and their own successful, community-supporting businesses.[28] Also during the 1970s, other regional and radical groups appeared – each with their distinctive emphases. Thanks to the vision of its Methodist leader, John Vincent, the few community houses of the Ashram Community cohered around the work of the Sheffield Inner City Ecumenical Mission and the closely related Urban Theology Unit. The congregations of SICEM and the Ashram Community developed ministries around eating together, such as the Eucharist congregation which began life in a city-centre restaurant on Sunday lunchtimes. The short, residential courses of the Urban Theology Unit were often predicated as we cooked and ate together.[29]

From its 1980s beginnings, one of the growing 'mission tools' of the English-speaking church has been the formulaic *Alpha* course. Its core components are a shared meal, a didactic talk and an interactive discussion group. Brevity precludes detailed critique here. However, many commentators attribute its success to the friendship-building shared meal and the fact that folk are encouraged to share their opinions in the discussion group.[30] Perhaps it is not so surprising in a post-modern world, with an increasing number of single-person households, that a shared meal and conversation declare both a welcoming hospitality while engendering a sense of community, however short-term.

In the twentieth century's final quarter, a whole genre of Christian books with titles ranging from *The Sheep that Got Away*[31] to *A Churchless Faith*[32] suggested that the number and frequency of church leavers were becoming too great to ignore. A recurring criticism from these 'dechurched' folks was that 'the church' was too big, over-demanding and impersonal, without any real sense of community or commitment to its founder's (Jesus') vision. Churchgoing was now perceived as a cumbersome extra which neither the individual nor wider society viewed as normative or necessary. Christendom was on the wane.

By the end of the 1980s, there had been another wave or resurgence of interest in Celtic spirituality[33] – and its lessons for today's church. Whether it was the Celtic-style prayers of David Adam, the *Wild Goose* songs of the Iona Community, the rhythmic prayer cycles of the newly forming Northumbria Community, this spirituality spoke to those often frustrated by the traditionalism of denominational Christianity, typical of Christendom. One of the key lessons learned was that this spirituality also revolved around the everyday, the meal table and welcoming others in the name of Christ, creating new patterns of community.

Some of the dechurched, disappointed or divorced Roman Catholic Christians followed a parallel liturgical path towards the Orthodox Church, which had existed in Britain within small diaspora groups, such as Russians, Greeks and Serbs. Others found their way via travel in the Greek islands or the music of the Orthodox composer, John Tavener. The Orthodox shrine at Walsingham reports increasing numbers of pilgrims, as do many Orthodox-based retreat house communities. There is a resurgence of those wishing to share temporarily in their worship and community, including the shared meals, whether overnight or for weekends.

Hospitality and community are both important and travel hand-in-hand.

Alongside this, small liturgical autocephalic Orders and congregations began to be noticed afresh. One of the groups of the independent Holy Celtic Church is the orthodox, Trinitarian, Order of Dionysis and Paul which, after their weekly Friday-evening liturgy, share supper together and brunch after their weekly Sunday-morning Mass.[34] The interest in 'order' and the 'new monasticism' has led the UK's Anabaptist Network and the Northumbria Community, in recent years, to jointly sponsor a series of well-attended day conferences; worship and eating together has been central to both their programme and findings.

From the 1990s, a growing symbiotic influence within both the Anabaptist Network and the Northumbria Community has been the growth in numbers of their respective nationwide supporters.[35] Like both the Ashram and Iona communities before them, these two newer groups have also developed semi-independent regional supporter groups which have met frequently – initially for prayer and study. However, all these four groups now recognize that the majority of their supporter groups also share a meal – as a sign of their communal life. Commentators often refer to these dispersed communities as 'network communities'. But all these four have members increasingly interested in shared households, indicating a desire for more intensive community.

Fresh Expressions

By the turn of the millennium, other more localized expressions of church were appearing; the denominational Fresh Expressions movement sought to learn from such 'gatherings'. Few regarded themselves as 'church' in any traditionalist or Christendom sense. Whether they met in homes, a café or community premises, they had no defining pattern except that the vast majority reported that the 'sharing of food' was instrumental to the way they met. This common characteristic is all the more important as studies of these 'emerging churches' reveal that many do not sing together and most do not meet on a Sunday.[36]

Such Fresh Expressions declare that grass-roots localism is important. In recent years, two Anabaptist-oriented 'expressions', operating at the grass-roots, have been planned more strategically. The first is Urban Expression,[37] planting self-supporting missional households in urban contexts. This is a fragile initiative, with no guarantees of success, but it is growing sufficiently to have developed the much appreciated Crucible training course.[38] The second is even younger – the Radix Community,[39] a mixture of Anabaptists and Jesus-centric Quakers. They are committed to shared households, eco-justice, peacemaking and neighbourhood activism. Both Urban Expression and Radix households extend hospitality several times each week.

Obviously, it is far too early to judge how these emerging churches will evolve or what place they will hold in the longer-term spectrum after Christendom further disintegrates. The same caveats must be applied to household networks, modelled on the Acts 2 and 4 patterns of Ashram, Columban and Catholic Worker households.

So What . . .?

Many of these groups, communities and networks attracted supporters beyond their local radius and roots. They have all developed regional supporter groups which resonate with the life and ethos of their 'parent'. What is difficult to judge is whether the marks of hospitality and community were deliberately adopted or whether these are the natural wellspring of Christians committed to something much more than Sunday denominational Christianity – and needing to eat or stay over when they gather.

The biblical witness suggests it is that 'wellspring' which becomes part of the fabric of the initial visionary gathering. Yet it naturally weaves into succeeding groups as they accept the high commitment level of the original vision. That vision is always rooted in the welcoming yet prophetic style of Jesus and his fluid, travelling band of disciples who prefigured the community of the kingdom.

The life of the pre-Christendom church and then that of the radical alternative-styled Christianity in the Christendom era point to similar conclusions. Just as Jesus and his disciples could not have undertaken itinerant preaching and teaching without the hospitality and community of committed supporters, neither could Waldo, Francis, the first Anabaptist leaders, English Dissenting preachers, George Fox, Restorationist evangelists and others.

The Iona and Northumbria communities in their mother houses – the former in Columban houses – the Ashram Community, the Catholic Worker and Jesus Fellowship households, alongside most of the regional Ashram, Iona, Northumbrian and Anabaptist Network supporter groups, all developed patterns of shared meals (many with table liturgies) as an expression of mutual hospitality and as a sign of community. Add in the witness of emerging churches, and there are enough evidential examples to invite our further exploration. This should include the practice of hospitality and involvement in shared meals, which lead to a renewed sense of community.

What makes all this seem different, to many churchgoers, is the fact that the practice is counter to the predominant culture of the inherited Christendom denominations. After Christendom, Christianity is recovering that New Testament counter-cultural stance. Christine Pohl's work demonstrates that historically the 'Local Christian communities shared meals together as part of their regular church practice – an important location for hospitality'.[40]

As the Church discovers its own place at the margins of soc-iety, it is rediscovering those New Testament practices which led to the explosive growth of Jesus' people in its earliest incarnations. It will ignore hospitality and shared meals at its peril.

The nature of Christian communities, whether in residential households, intimate congregations or 'dispersed', will be diverse and untidy.[41] It will beg the question: What is a proper church? It will not be a mandated form, determined by top-down denominational policies. It is far more likely to be a Spirit-led, grass-roots 'gathering' of those for whom Jesus is confessed not only as Saviour but also as Lord in the sense of life-example and compass point.

What is also clear is that hospitality, eating together and some form of community life increasingly marks Christianity after Christendom, echoing the counter-cultural 'norms' which developed centuries before and as the radical alternative during Christendom.

4

Gathering at the Table

On a beautiful April Sunday on Iona, the penny finally dropped. Only the day before, I had led a disparate group from my Leeds parish to spend a week's study-holiday while living as part of the residential Iona Community.

We went to that Sunday's Holy Communion in a packed Iona Abbey. The presiding minister, dressed in a Fair Isle jersey, tore the huge loaf. He then invited us to share our bread with another person in the rebuilt historic cloister. I shared mine with a Spanish-speaker from a Chicago housing project while an Edinburgh lecturer shared her bread with me. There on Iona, the core residential group through their worship, welcome and hospitality ensured that even passing visitors and short-term guests became part of the community.

As our Leeds group gathered afterwards in the abbey library, to talk through our 'hopes for the week', we were given a bowl of leftover bread to share. Then over lunch, more wooden bowls of the leftover bread appeared on the refectory tables to accompany the bean soup. There was something reminiscent of gathering up the leftovers after Jesus had fed the multitude (Luke 9:10–17). That afternoon, we walked to a silvery beach, kicked off our hiking boots and reflected on the day.

All of us had made the connection between Holy Communion and the nature of community in similar ways. What we did at the Lord's table in worship had to affect the way we acted at every other table. That same God had provided those tables for us, too. 'Christians of all people should know that food shapes belief because their religion is defined by a dinner.'[1] Our various experiences of sharing Communion during that week meant we all left with questions about what we are celebrating and how we could do that more fully.

What's in a Name?

Both on Iona and in our Leeds parish, we happily referred to 'Holy Communion'; this term speaking to our broad ecumenical contacts. This is the service most often called 'the Lord's Supper' in the varied traditions of the Christian church. However, the term 'Eucharist'[2] is often used in historical and/or liturgical ecumenical writing. They are all variant names for Jesus' Last Supper with his disciples, on the night when he was betrayed unto death, hence that universal term – the Lord's Supper.

Within the more radical Christian traditions, this is often known as the 'Common Meal' or 'Shared Meal'. However, for the purposes of this volume, as I need to differentiate between those occasions when Christian groups meet to share in a meal, sharing bread and wine utilizing Jesus' words and intentions, from other shared-meal occasions, I will use Lord's Supper for the former and 'shared meal' for the latter. However, this is a very Christendom-like distinction as it implies there are occasions when Christians are acting in particular Jesus ways and the rest of the time there is a different compass point.

What Are We Celebrating?

Over many years, I have had the privilege of sharing the Lord's Supper in many contexts, from cathedrals to the shores of Galilee, in House Churches and at the bedsides of the dying. What does this experience mean – given these different contexts – particularly when Jesus says, 'Do this in remembrance of me' (Luke 22:19)?

The life-changing challenge of Jesus in his Jewish context and of radical, normally counter-cultural Christian communities has been highlighted in the previous chapters. What is central to them all is the life and ministry of Jesus, exemplifying a pattern for discipleship then and now. In this chapter's consideration of

Jesus, we need to retain the backdrop of the centrality of sharing meals both in his own life and the previous biblical (Hebrew) tradition.

However, this same Jesus, proclaimed by the mainstream church, seemed to gain a compartmentalized existence. Jesus' life was often constrained by the church's liturgy into a God of the Sunday gospel readings, the statements of the Creed and the liturgical seasons, such as:

- the Holy Child – the gift of the Virgin Birth,
- the miracle-working rabbi, whose work was portioned out by Sunday gospel snapshots,
- the sacrificial Saviour, whose death on the cross changed history,
- the Lord of Resurrection morning – an Easter God,
- the Ascended Lord of heaven and earth – the Christ in glory.

These are all true and attested by the New Testament narratives and the beliefs of countless martyrs, saints and faithful Christians through the ages. But it is not the whole story.

There is the very human Jesus at the heart of all this. This is the Jesus who laughed and wept;[3] the Jesus who ate with his friends and sinners. This Jesus, whom both theology and faith teach us about, is the human face of God. This Jesus is no plaster-cast Saviour.

This is the Jesus who invited himself to supper to the home of the collaborator Zacchaeus. This is the Jesus who rebuked the religious leaders who criticized the breaking of dietary laws by the disciples. This is the Jesus who shared out bread for the crowds when the sceptics doubted. This is the Jesus who ate a last Passover with his disciples in a borrowed upper room. This is the Jesus who gave new significance to what his followers should do with their bread and wine. This is a Jesus who called together a new community – his community. This is the Jesus who, gesturing to the shared bread and cup, said, 'Do this in remembrance of me' (Luke 22:19). This is the Jesus whom I know and have steered my life by for over forty years – and continue to do so.

As Christians gather, we need to ask: How are we gathering and celebrating the vibrancy of Jesus' intention? Eleanor Kreider, the Anabaptist liturgist and gifted worship leader, helpfully challenged the whole church to consider this perspective afresh in her 1997 book, *Communion Shapes Character*.[4] 'The Lord's table set in the middle of the congregation is a potent symbol of Christ's presence in the midst of his people. The very act of gathering around the table symbolizes and helps to make true the communion and unity the people experience.'[5] We must not let architecture, nor traditional church furniture, impede what we declare at the Lord's Supper.

If we are to be and be seen as Jesus' new community, enough of his life's pattern must be made evident in our sharing of anything and everything, and not just bread and wine.

Communion: the Ultimate Jesus Meal?

As Chapter 2 surveyed, the gospels are woven through with short episodes about Jesus and the disciples sharing food. Whether in joining Zacchaeus's household or in sharing a few loaves and fishes with a great crowd, both episodes demonstrate Jesus' desire to welcome and include others as they are fed.

The Synoptic Gospels of Matthew, Mark and Luke imply that Jesus and his disciples spent a few years together. A simple analysis of these gospel narratives suggests that Jesus spent about 25 per cent of his time teaching and preaching, another 25 per cent 'healing the sick' and a further 25 per cent in solitude, prayer and contemplation. The final 25 per cent are episodes concerning the sharing of food in a variety of contexts.[6]

This chapter's focus is upon one particular meal and what we learn from Jesus at the Last Supper. It is that Last Supper and what Jesus said and did then, which has not only provided the raw material but developed into the Christian practice of the Lord's Supper. This set a broader agenda for discipleship in the world.

The Jesus way

The Jewish Passover is celebrated annually. It is likely that Jesus and his disciples would have shared the Passover on a number of these annual occasions. John's Gospel appears to limit Jesus' public ministry to a few months, potentially arguing that Jesus and his disciples would have shared the Passover only once.[7] But John's Gospel conflates other events, suggesting its shortened timescale is a literary device.

The ceremonial words and actions of the gospel accounts of the Last Supper were part of the full Passover meal, in that borrowed upper room. Bread and wine would naturally be upon the table in sufficient quantity to share.[8] Adult Jewish men would know the Passover ritual and words as a special part of their life's fabric. It would be only with hindsight – when Jesus had been betrayed, tried, tortured then crucified – that the significance of all that had occurred could even start to become apparent.

John's Gospel tells the events of the Last Supper differently. In John 13 Jesus washed the disciples' feet (vv. 1–17) and Jesus' identification of his betrayer as 'the one to whom I will give this piece of bread when I have dipped it in the dish' is recorded (v. 26). It is the Synoptic Gospels (and Paul in 1 Cor. 11:23–5) that provide us with accounts of the sharing of bread and wine. Biblical commentators will continue to argue over the *ipsissima verba*, the actual words of Jesus, but what is clear is that the Synoptic Gospels note the *ipsissima vox*, the actual voice and way of Jesus. Discipleship is about following the way of Jesus and letting his voice be heard through us. To be disciples, we need to make those connections in our own practice today.

Jesus did imbue the sharing of bread and the sharing of wine, in the context of that meal, with particular significance. The everyday Aramaic language of Galileans made minimal use of verbs. It is later Greek, Latin and English translators of the Bible who struggle to represent Jesus' meaning as he took the bread, blessed and broke it before offering it. His words then told how this represented his about-to-be-broken body. The literal Aramaic is: 'This my body.' Translators had the same linguistic difficulties with Jesus' words about the cup of wine; Jesus would have said: 'This my blood.'

Tragically, too much theological argument can destroy the nature of what those words can mean. But blinkered by such arguments, the meal context which Jesus utilizes to make those connections is also lost.

Whatever Jesus did and said at that Last Supper, his way of hosting was so powerful that, days later, his similar actions as the unknown pilgrim who broke the bread at the Emmaus table made his companions realize this was the Risen Lord (Luke 24:13–35).

What the church did

Both Luke's use of 'the breaking of bread' as a specific occasion in Acts 2:46 and Paul's writing to the gathered Corinthian Christians (1 Cor. 11) tell us that the practice of Communion was a natural part of the New Testament church. Academic studies and more accessible accounts[9] seek to emphasize this.

Sufficient archaeological and academic research shows that the sharing of bread and wine, as Jesus commanded, was part of an everyday meal.[10] Most writers trace this back to the New Testament communities of first Christian converts. 'This meal is vital, for as the members of the community eat and drink together their unity comes to visible expression.'[11] Here, Banks recognizes the role of the whole meal as part of the community's building. To so share demands both a place and hospitable host.

Extant historical documents, from the second century, show the development of Communion as a central rite of the growing Christian community.[12] From third-century (and later) monasticism, the only time some groups fully met together was for a weekly meal which included Holy Communion. In the face of persecution, rituals (like Communion) both provided a community with identity and helped bind it together.

What Christendom did

After the fourth-century legalization of Christianity, the church naturally grew. Christendom's need for both orthodoxy and consistent practice rapidly became greater. Liturgical historians can trace the development of Communion rituals, with their set formats called liturgies and the demand that only officially ordained priests lead such services. Everyone *had* to be baptized as a Christian within the empire. This became law in AD 529 under Emperor Justinian. Logic then assumes everyone was automatically part of the official church. Therefore, they did not need to eat together in church, nor live in community together.

Historically, the Lord's Supper in mainstream Christendom was reduced to set services using ritual actions and responses, as well as miniscule amounts of bread and wine. This pattern is still recognizable now in the vast majority of more traditional Sunday congregations. During Christendom centuries, only authorized clergy could preside at Communion.

Radical alternative Christian ways

However, over the centuries, many of the radical alternative Christian movements have continued to share Communion as part of a meal and other associated practices of Jesus; for example, some Anabaptist groups incorporated foot-washing too.

For fourteenth-century Waldensians in the Italian Alps, sixteenth-century Anabaptists across northern Europe and later centuries' English Dissenters, their persecutors could accuse them of having a meal only if they were discovered together around a spread meal table. So sharing a meal was true to Jesus' example and bound them together as a community despite threat, opposition and persecution. Sharing a Communion meal continued to declare their communal faith.

Twenty-first-century ways for Communion

The manner in which twenty-first-century Christians share in services of the Lord's Supper tells us both of their individual faith and piety as well as the official understanding that their church holds. Whether these groups include a meal says something of their theology.

The nature of what we do today is still shaped by erudite theological words, often Greek or Latin, which are loaded with inherent meaning and symbolism yet are not understood by many who gather at the table.

'It's all Greek to me!'

For some years, I was part of a congregation which used to tell the Communion narrative spontaneously at its monthly Sunday-evening Communion. Rather than the presiding minister reading Paul's narrative of Jesus' Communion from the Bible (1 Cor. 11:23–29), that minister would invite the congregation to tell the whole story to one another. The various responses made this multi-voiced, enabling interjection from others to add further detail. The story came alive as the people rehearsed for themselves why they were to share Holy Communion together. One pensioner told me: 'Before we started doing that, it was all Greek to me.'

His comment was more perceptive than he realized. It provides both this section's title and an indication of how issues of Latin and Greek interpretation have been stumbling-blocks to both Christian unity and personal discipleship.

The practice of today's church is rooted in a time when arguments about theology and faith could hinge on semantic arguments about Greek or Latin. An orthodox understanding of Jesus' Incarnation was hammered out in AD 451 at the Council of Chalcedon; this was also dependent upon interpretation of Greek linguistic nuances.

The division of the eastern and western church in 1054 was also a matter of different Latin interpretations of the Creed. The Reformation in the sixteenth century occurred because of differences over papal authority and the right of individuals to use neither the Latin Bible (e.g. Martin Luther translated the New Testament into German) nor the Latin Mass.

Regrettably, many schemes for uniting Christian communities in different parts of the world have faltered on their different understandings about Holy Communion or whether a priest must preside. As these communities have talked, their leaders and theologians have realized that words and concepts from those past separations still have power to control Communion practice today. In looking afresh at three of those Greek concepts, we can identify both that power and their ability to enable desirable change if taken seriously today.

Greek concepts for desirable change

Leitourgia – the work of the people

In this chapter, the word 'liturgy' has been used to describe the form of the service, including the words, actions and responses used at particular Communion services. The word 'liturgy' is the English version of the Greek word *leitourgia*, which means 'work of the people'. Originally, *leitourgia* referred to a charitable action, often by a specific individual, giving something for the use of the whole community. Gradually, the word was applied to ritual occasions in which a number of people participated, such as Christian worship.

Contrasting this, by the late twentieth century, church worship had seemed no longer to be the 'work of the people'. Most UK Anglican and Roman Catholic services of the Lord's Supper are led by a single priest, with some set responses and bidding prayers. A similar clerical dominance is true of Free Churches and many newer churches as well.

If Christianity is not to be denigrated as some erudite sect, with its knowledge in the minds and voices of a few, then it must recover that 'work of the people' as the pattern for much of its public worship. The example of a congregation telling the Communion narrative piecemeal between them is a step in the right direction. The ecumenical, central-Swindon congregation brings forward the loaf of bread, the jug of wine and their monetary collection simultaneously as a symbol of bringing together all God's gifts. Another congregation in Kent, whose building enables worship in-the-round, does the same but brings each gift from a different compass-point direction, symbolizing that the whole congregation is bringing forward the gifts involved.

The work of the people is more than the words which are said, or the biblical narratives locally retold, or the recognition that worship must involve movement and participation. It is about the empowerment of the people.

A minister of four small struggling congregations agreed she would lead each congregation on one Sunday morning per month. By her third month as their minister, she asked each congregation on its Sunday to bring food to share after worship. The minister facilitated each congregation to begin redefining how they would like to share together in leading worship. After only a year, all the congregations have grown and two have doubled in size.

Each of these four congregations made changes in their worship. Some changes were simple, such as sitting in semi-circles, or local church members leading *all* the prayers. All four congregations enabled their members to feel more comfortable about inviting their friends. For them, worship and mission are once again the 'work of the people'. Without being explicit, what happened was a rediscovery of both hospitality and community.

Anamnesis – past, present and future

At the Lord's Supper we retell the Jesus story (past) in today's worship (present) and look forward (future) to the great banquet of the kingdom. The technical word *anamnesis* indicates rich remembering which focuses not only on something that happened in the past, but a past event being recalled in the present which serves as a foretaste of the future. We do not need to used the word *anamnesis* but we do need to recognize the reality it points to.

Some years ago, a dying neighbour with whom I had shared the Lord's Supper told me she found great comfort in that we had done what Jesus did at the Last Supper. She was certain that we would meet again at the 'great banquet of heaven' – her chosen phrase. Ever since that long vigil at her bedside, I can never share those gifts of bread and wine with others without remembering her words. Now I easily recognize that past-present-future moment which is *anamnesis*.

At seminary, I grew to love the adapted simplicity of a Methodist post-Communion prayer in plain English:

> We thank you Lord, that you have fed us in this sacrament,
> united us with Christ
> and given us a foretaste of the heavenly banquet
> prepared for all your people.[13]

As a parish minister, I used that prayer to end each week's Communion. Those simple words tell us of what we have just shared, uniting us with the action of Jesus the Messiah at that Last Supper, while heralding the banquet which my dying neighbour knew was promised to us all.

Epiclesis – come, Holy Spirit

While training for ordained ministry, a group of us undertook a pilgrimage to Lindisfarne, Northumberland's Holy Island. After several days of walking, some began a discussion about whether we could have Communion on this long march.

We replayed an argument that echoed across the centuries and had caused many Christian divisions. My Roman Catholic and Anglican fellow-pilgrims asserted that only an ordained priest may say the necessary invocation of the Holy Spirit to ensure Communion's ritual validity. That invocation is known as the *epiclesis*. My friends from these two traditions could not agree in recognizing each other's priestly orders. Surely God is not selectively deaf, as though only blessing bread and wine when a priest invites the gift of the Spirit?

What makes the words 'Come, Holy Spirit' effective in the Communion service? It is the beliefs and expectations of the assembled faithful disciples. Whatever form of words is used, what is important is that the Holy Spirit will also 'work' in the hearts and minds of the people. It is not what occurs in the bread and wine that validates Communion. It is the work of the Spirit drawing participants into God's fuller presence.

In the Anglican Communion liturgy, there is a suggestion to use three prayers. These prayers follow a similar pattern and wording; the first is as we offer the bread, the second in offering the wine and the third prayer says:

> Blessed are you, Lord God, King of the Universe,
> through your goodness, we have ourselves to offer,
> fruit of the womb and work of your Holy Spirit,
> blessed are You for ever.[14]

Perhaps the true *epiclesis* can occur when we recognize that God is continuing to work within us, both as individuals and as a community of faith, every time we take seriously Jesus' own agenda in sharing bread and wine.

'Thou preparest a table before me'

These traditional words from Psalm 23 (AV) tell us of God's provision even 'in the presence of mine enemies' so that 'my cup runneth over'. This is a psalm that affirms God's promise to all his people. Therefore, whatever the circumstances, God will provide, even in the face of adversity but with such sufficiency that there will be more than enough. The gospel narrative of Jesus feeding the great crowds with loaves and fishes declares that the divine promise continues.

My experience of back-packing through the Greek islands brought me into contact with peasant communities. Several were too poor to sustain even a bar or public café in the village. Yet so often, after enquiry in my broken, faltering Greek, a family would invite me to eat with them. Bread and some robust wine were the staples, alongside home-grown tomatoes and olives and occasionally cheese from their own goats. From their poverty, their invitation was full and the fare rich.

Nearly everyone values generous table hospitality, however simple the food, sharing what is available. This is the biblical image which Jesus instigated, the early Church nurtured, Paul explained and Christians today still follow as they share Holy Communion. So what does it mean to acknowledge that there is bread for all as we drink the wine of the kingdom, gathering as its new community?

Bread for all

Two of the distinguishing marks of the Jewish Passover are its hospitality, within the community, and the welcome to the stranger who will be fed. At the Passover table there is bread for all. That would have been an unquestioning understanding for Jesus and his disciples. They knew generosity, hospitality and welcome as they gathered in that borrowed but already prepared upper room, to share that final Passover, which we know now as the Last Supper.

The God we know in Jesus has prepared this table and determined what we should do at it. So, we declare that at this table there will be bread for all. This is our inherited understanding from both Passover and the book of Psalms. This generosity is also a prophetic statement. It echoes God's provision of manna in the wilderness. It evokes the Spirit increasing what little there was at the widow's table so she, her family and the prophet were fed (1 Kgs 17:7ff.).

That threefold acceptance of Passover, psalm and prophet is the basis of Hebrew theology: all declaring there will be bread for all when God is at work among his people, who gather at the table in his name.

Jesus' own teaching is of the kingdom of God. This is about the reign of God, not earthly territory. Jesus' teaching of the kingdom, in both word and action, is of bread for all – whether through miracle or sharing hospitality. 'Jesus expressed gratuitousness in his inclusive table fellowship. The table of blessing is for all, those who can pay and those who cannot.'[15]

The kingdom cannot be the kingdom of God unless wrongs are righted. A great injustice of our time is that there are those who starve and go hungry while others eat in abundance. We Christians with our plenty should acknowledge the kingdom's demand that we work to change that inequality so that there will be bread for all. Hospitality and justice also travel together.

It is no accident that Holy Communion is described as the foretaste of the feast of the kingdom. As that precursor, it must prefigure through both word and action that reign of God when there is bread for all. In that moment of Holy Communion, Jesus makes us equals and we cannot walk away from that moment leaving our sisters and brothers to go hungry.

John Howard Yoder, the Mennonite theologian, said, 'Bread eaten together *is* economic sharing . . . That basic needs are met is a sign of the messianic age.'[16] 'Do this in remembering me', said Jesus, as he broke the loaf and shared it with everyone at the table. The kingdom does not have second-class citizens. If there are hungry ones, we have not seen Jesus in them; 'Lord, when did we see you hungry?' (Matt. 25:37). Eating at Jesus' table, and remembering him, means that there will bread for all if we but hear his words afresh.

The wine of the kingdom

Both in Israel and in Britain, I have learned much from sharing in Passover meals with Jewish friends and neighbours. As each occasion drew to its close, we lifted our glasses of wine and said, 'Next year, Jerusalem'. In this phrase, there was both a desire and anticipation to share this meal afresh in the place that was their focus of God's promise. 'Next year, Jerusalem' is a transformative toast, changing priorities so that from today, a new reality for the future can occur.

When I was child, it seemed to me that only the aristocracy and James Bond seemed to have wine with meals each day. As a teenager, I learned to appreciate both my parents' teetotal lives and an occasional glass of wine at special meals in other homes. Against this background, wine gained significance as the drink of celebration. My growing understanding of the Last Supper's example taught me this.

The gospel images of water-into-wine (John 2:1–11) and of new wineskins (Mark 2:18–22) became favourite preaching examples and not just at weddings and congregational relaunches respectively. The concept that new wine was transformative is important. Whether through a miracle or natural reaction, the presence and use of wine makes a difference beyond everyday expectations.

While some may rejoice, many in Free Church congregations are disturbed by the use of Ribena, or some proprietary non-alcoholic Communion wine or worse as the substitute for wine at their Communion services. Many are also disturbed with the use of individual tiny glasses despite the best theologizing which purports that this prefigures the kingdom – all drinking equally and together at one time. In these two struggles, there is a recognition that diminishing what Jesus advocated (i.e. using the wine of the table and drinking from the common cup), diminishes what is being celebrated.

Despite Paul's warning to the Corinthian church against drunken carousing at the Lord's Supper, the sharing of wine among the believers at Communion needs to be a celebration. It needs to anticipate the kingdom that is coming and that will be celebrated at the Great King's feast. It needs to help participants recognize that the sharing of a cup of wine has a significance beyond any everyday meal. One of the best contemporary hymns invites us to share that new wine of the kingdom. Normally, one serves the best wine to family and friends and other invited guests and not some poor second-class substitute. If we choose to offer the second-best, what are we saying about the fullness of the invitation or how much they are valued?

The community of the kingdom

The meaning and purpose of the gathering at the table was finally brought home to me while living in rural France – but not from a Christian congregation. Each autumn, one of our neighbours would assemble his motley network of family, friends and neighbours for the grape-harvest or *vendange*.

We would gather in his yard shortly after 7.00 a.m., when the mist lay heavy over the land. Large loaves of bread were passed around; everyone tore their own hunk, and washed it down with a large glass of strong red wine. Locally, this was known as the *casse-croute*, literally the 'breaking of bread'. Whether we laboured under hot sun or chilling autumn rain, we could pause for a good lunch but could not rest until the last vineyard was stripped of its grapes. That evening, this same neighbour hosted a banquet of many courses, where every worker, young and old, was welcomed.

The parable became evident. The commitment to our shared task was declared and toasted at the *casse-croute*. This group of people had come together at the invitation of one person – the neighbour who owned the vineyard. All he could promise was to provide for us in that day's task and journey before letting us all enjoy the great banquet in his barn at the end of the day. Gospel images flooded my thinking: the vineyard and its owner, the breaking of bread, the wine, and the promised banquet.

As we stumbled home through the darkness from the *vendange*, the Christians reflected upon its theology for each of us.

When we are 'gathering at Christ's table, our life is shaped by the food and etiquette of that table. But it is at that table that we learn the table etiquette. Faith creates morality. It is not the other way round. The invitation to the table is unconditional. That is the freedom we feast on in Christ.'[17] Our words may not have been as eloquent as Campbell's but this summary helped us recognize how much more we had found during our day in the vineyard than in many of our Christian experiences. Our host's generous hospitality echoed that of Jesus and called for a committed voluntary and active response.

Recognizing that Moment

Before moving on, I need to acknowledge the cries of my biblical scholar-friends who concur with the work of John Dominic Crossan. In his seminal book, *The Historical Jesus: The Life of a*

Mediterranean Jewish Peasant,[18] he posits the view that the early church practised a bread-and-fish (rather than bread-and-wine) Eucharist (Crossan's preferred term). None of this destroys any of the present chapter's trajectory, although it might diminish the power of the 'wine of celebration' image. Powerfully, it underpins the fact that early church celebrations of the Lord's Supper would therefore have formed part of a full meal. This required someone's hospitality – a fact from which Crossan does not demur.

Later in this book, there are short stories telling of small communities of Jesus' kingdom, who are not just Sunday congregations. Often they have gathered purposefully. Each such group knows that it is their response to a part of Jesus' own invitation which has brought them together. For all those groups and their stories, it is the shared meal and breaking bread together which helps them constitute themselves as a community of the kingdom.

Whether it is in the history of the early church or in those radical non-mainstream Christian movements, the common task and shared meal helps define them as communities of the kingdom.[19] In an increasingly secularized world, which marginalizes Christianity, every group or congregation which knows Jesus at its centre is having to face up to the questions:

- How do we become such a community of the kingdom? How we exercise eucharistic hospitality and the nature of its celebration will say much about our community of faith, even if it is only a Sunday congregation.
- Is our group committed to the politic of the kingdom's bread for all?
- How do our meal practices, our Communion, prefigure the great and final banquet?

5

Hospitality Creates Community

How we offer hospitality, as individuals, as families, as Jesus communities, says a lot about us. It also affects the people we are, socially and spiritually. Hospitality makes a theological statement. It also says what kind of community we live and believe in, as well as aspire to and want to share.

Hospitality shapes not only the life of those who accept an invitation to a meal. Hospitality reshapes the group that makes the invitation. As folks respond with thanks and/or gracious compliments, hosts can easily reflect how little they have done relatively, yet what a big effect has been made. The nature of shared hospitality shapes the ways in which we interrelate – how we become some form of community. Hospitality helps to create community. Christians need to gather up these reflections properly and realize what this is saying to us.

Hospitality and its meaning have shaped my life. It has also built a form of extended family – a form of community. It is in various groups that I share ideas, laughter, life and faith as we share meals, time together, weekend breaks, holidays and neighbourhood activism. One of my newer friends, after sharing a meal with others in my home, said that he felt like he had been with Jesus' disciples. A rich and real compliment, particularly as he is not a believer. If ever there was a manifesto moment for hospitality, that was it.

After a lifetime of sharing in Christian ministry, I am convinced that contemporary, radical Jesus communities (which others sometimes belittle as simply congregations) need to actively address their understanding of hospitality. It does shape the nature of their community, as well as their spirituality.

Blessed Beginnings

I was blessed to grow up in family and Christian environments where hospitality was and still is the norm. Some of my earliest family memories are being sat around happy meal tables or visiting others where food and joyful conversation predominate the recall. Camping with school-friends, beer and barbecues with workmates, shared households and supper parties all form part of my life's scenery. Not everyone has that blessing. For them, we must ensure that the Jesus community chooses to be a model of a new social order.

As a child, I witnessed my grandfather inviting every visitor to his church's Sunday morning worship back home for lunch, addressing every man as 'Brother'. As a 4 year old, I remember Ivan telling me of his homestead and family back in Jamaica. On a lonely second Sunday in Britain, Ivan had wandered into that church and, following Grandpa's invitation, had been for lunch with my grandparents on every Sunday since. My grandmother always told me: 'Make sure there is food and space at your table when you grow up.' A good lesson to learn.

Time's distance precludes real assessment of the effect of my grandparents' hospitality on that congregation. But that congregation grew into being one of Birmingham's first fully integrated mixed-race congregations. Note: the congregation grew. My grandparents' home was always full of visitors, laughter and vibrant conversation. Lifelong friendships were forged. After my grandfather's death, Ivan came every Sunday to drive my grandmother, my sister and me to 'our' church; that same church never met socially without there being food-in-plenty.

Over the years, I have been privileged to receive a lot of gracious and generous hospitality – wherever I have travelled. Whether the hosts and givers have been people of faith or of none, a bond has been forged. In each instance of those relationships, a vision of community, however transient, was both created and celebrated. We can glimpse something of a world that is bigger than what exists in the temporal moment.

To enable our present reflection upon how hospitality may shape the Jesus community, its (and our) theology and spirituality, let me offer you a contemporary congregational example. Later I will share some more of those intervening years. Here is the story of a local congregation that learned about hospitality and was shaped by it.

Emmanuel – a Local Church Shaped by Hospitality

We had just spent many months living in France, renovating a derelict barn into a retreat house. We had been called away from ministry in Kent, to pursue a 'prayer – study – work – hospitality' vocation.

This echoed the centuries-old Benedictine communal monastic practice. Our many visitors had enjoyed sun-drenched lunches on our terrace as well as quiet prayerful moments in our stone-built village house.

One of our guests kept insisting that God was giving her the word 'Swindon' for our future. When we returned to the UK, the United Reformed Church invited me to consider becoming the minister at Emmanuel, Haydon Wick, on the growing northern edge of Swindon.

Discerning together

Emmanuel was a small but dynamic congregation. Its eldership team were hungry to discern a new vision and direction for their mission. Their very practical buildings are set within their own orchard, at the edge of the old village. This congregation had a history of good hospitality. In the past, it had served as a focus of encouragement to all the villagers to share the surplus produce of their gardens and allotments. At the heart of Emmanuel were two vibrant Sunday congregations, who wanted worship to be accessible for all ages. They wanted to use as many talents, gifts and voices as possible.

They welcomed me as their minister. The preacher at that welcome service used the images of hospitality in the New Testament church from Acts 2 and of leadership in the breakfast barbecue of John 21 as two core themes. After a further three hours of conversation, laughter and good food, I felt it was like coming home.

Ministry with that eldership always felt simply a God-given privilege to spend my life upon. I used to tell them that. Gradually, we built up a new pattern of multi-voiced worship as well as trust between those who simply worshipped together on Sundays.

More than Sundays

Harvest Festival was a real offering of home-grown produce, jams and chutneys as well as tokens of Christian gifts, everyday skills, crafts and hobbies. On the Sunday evening before Christmas, the landlady of the Fox and Hounds pub nearby happily allowed us to lead carol singing – our pints in hand – while she served free mince pies and satsumas. Worship on the Sunday after Christmas was always informal – we gathered around a piano for more carols before sharing our leftovers but definitely no more turkey! One of my weekly priorities was to join the Lunch Club team, cooking and serving lunch on Thursdays to over forty retired folks.

Our annual church meeting, with only a handful attending, had become dry-as-dust so we changed it. We decided to meet on a Saturday teatime, welcoming children and ensuring lifts for the infirm, serving a main meal with dessert for allcomers. Folk sat around tables set for eight so they could be asked to chat about policies and ideas informally between courses. Then over coffee and mints, each of the twelve or so tables also devised a question to ask the minister, who had only a minute to answer each of their questions.

Residential church weekends had priced themselves beyond most of our families. So we used the early May Bank Holiday for a non-residential version. After a Saturday full of diverse seminars and activities, with a bring-and-share lunch, people invited others for tea before a planned variety of evening social gatherings in homes. We spent Sunday together between morning and evening worship, when I led a few of the catering team to provide a full cooked Sunday lunch for everyone, including first-time visitors, and then afternoon tea and cake. On the Bank Holiday Monday, the church hired a large coach as we went out for a picnic at a prearranged venue, stopping for cake, juice cartons and worship on the way home.

New beginnings

The real key to the congregation's growth was to feed them, both spiritually and physically. Over lunch at an elders' away-day, I revealed the results of a congregational survey. Our congregation really enjoyed eating together and felt comfortable enough to bring their non-believing friends along. The elders had by then done a lot of praying, enough Bible study and enough visiting to discern that strategically our small-group programme needed to reflect this.

We relaunched our fortnightly home-based groups, for prayer, care and Bible study. Only now, each group would share a meal beforehand (since then one morning group has changed to sharing lunch afterwards). Over 50 per cent of the membership signed up for the first set of groups. Two groups have now multiplied to allow more to join as others came into the church. Each group chooses how the food is provided for and who it is cooked by. Happily there is none of that competition I have known in the dinner-party circuit or one sees on TV dining programmes.

What they learned spilled over into mission. Food was a great gatherer of people. Autumn Fairtrade chocolate parties were successful in selling both Christmas presents and Jesus' ideas about justice. Open-air, summer-monthly, Sunday-afternoon *Songs of Praise*-type events, with cream teas in the orchard, gathered crowds and faith enquiries. One elder, a canoe instructor, led men canoeing upriver to a sausage sizzle, where the talk easily moved to Jesus.

Sadly all good things come to an end. In spring 2007, a virus put me in hospital with a diagnosis of a terminal heart condition. Thanks to answered prayers, I survived. Rejoice – in my absence, the church grew, as did the elders' gifts, as did the number of home groups. Eventually I had to retire on the grounds of ill health. Subsequently, they have developed a monthly Sunday-lunch-for-all, with an evolving pattern. All this demonstrates that the congregation understood Christian hospitality is central to their way of following Jesus together. No surprise really as *Emmanuel* means 'God with us'.

My successor as minister has had the pastoral wisdom to encourage the development of those lay-led meal-based home groups, multi-voiced worship and meals as central to mission. The latest I have heard is that they are planning to rebuild and enlarge their building's kitchen and publish a booklet with prayers on one page and recipes on the page opposite.

Reshaping the Church

Emmanuel never really fell into the trap of many well-meaning Christian conferences and congregations posing questions about whether we 'do church' or should 'be church'. Most folk just got on comfortably with the fact they were part of the 'Jesus community'. Their thinking was shaped more by the acceptance that we are sharing a faith journey with Jesus, rather than some chapter-and-verse mentality about Scripture or needing to have a fixation about when you were saved.

Having said all that, the Emmanuel congregation would want me to say that they have their faults and they are fallible people – so it has been said. However, their experience was untypical enough to become the congregational research substrate for my doctoral studies.

We need to rethink our ideas about church, as Emmanuel continues to do, recognizing that we will not arrive in this life but remain on the journey. Christianity is a pilgrim faith, rooted in following Jesus. As Jesus ate each Sabbath eve with his family or friends, they too declared, 'My father was a wandering Aramean.' If we can learn anything from radical church history (see Chapter 3), it is that we are following the Jesus who told us, 'Foxes have holes and birds of the air have nests, but the Son of Man has nowhere to lay his head' (Matt. 8:20).

A pilgrim theology: learning hospitality from others

In recent, separate contexts, several conversations with the Iona Community's leader and a Taizé Community brother confirm the need to be constantly reviewing our practices of hospitality and community. Both spoke eloquently of how much their respective communities gain from the way in which their members travel to live temporarily (whether for days or years) elsewhere – sometimes in tiny proto-communities or households set in difficult locations. Again that echoes the lessons of the radicals of church history. Explicitly, once we step out beyond the norms of organized patterns, in the way and name of Jesus, new things happen.

This is not just a personal flight of fancy. In the British ecumenical movement, a recent dominant motif has been that we are 'Not Strangers, but Pilgrims'. This has been explored during several Lent courses. A former Bishop of Warrington in the 1980s was one of the first establishment voices to question whether the church should be 'pioneers' or 'settlers'. That bishop indicated that most Anglican congregations were indeed the latter. It is hardly surprising that one of the New Church networks had already adopted the Pioneer name.

While the concepts of uncharted territory, the 'wild west' and post- (After) Christendom may not seem coterminous, they have much in common. If we know anything about pioneers and pilgrims, it is that they shared all their resources including food, often eating together as they undertook their journey.

Whether we choose to learn from Pullman's *Dark Materials* trilogy, Tolkien's *Lord of the Rings*, Bunyan's *Pilgrim's Progress* or even the Bible, the understanding that the journey is central to the discovery of the ultimate truth is common to them all. The members of my neighbourhood book group are predominantly non-Christian yet we always eat together, finding it then far easier to talk about the first two trilogies' questions. Christians have to learn how and where to pitch their missiological tent – to share more bread than talk, in this journey after Christendom. No longer can the church presume familiarity with its literature base but must build relationships towards the new community with what is common to all – food and hospitality.

Whether in north Africa or the remoter Greek islands, I encountered hospitality being offered to me as I hiked my way. Food-sharing and journeying are integrally bound.

Spirituality of hospitality: grace and simplicity and justice

Whether a household says 'grace' before eating tells of its spirituality. Celtic Christians supposedly had prayers for everything, including lighting the fire, milking the cow and table graces, ensuring that everyday life and prayer were interwoven. Sharing meals with Taizé brothers or while staying at Iona Abbey, I am always struck by the inherent power of the song, the silence or the eloquent words that act as grace at each meal. Joining hands around the table in Amish, Bruderhof, Mennonite and Radix households during grace reminds me of the visionary community we are prefiguring in sharing food. If we believe God is our provider, can we not demonstrate it with such simplicity as followers of Jesus?

The work of Canadian theologian, Christine Pohl, has encouraged many not just to explore but to rediscover hospitality as an essential Christian practice. As she rightly comments, 'Because hospitality is basic to who we are as followers of Jesus, every aspect of our lives can be touched by its practice.'[1] Spirituality should engender a simplicity of life. In both monastic and radical Christian households, there is normally a simplicity of diet – both at the meal table and in prayer.

Recently I stayed in one such small community,[2] where single futons line the long wall of the largest upstairs bedroom. Twice each day, that room's corner 'prayer station' – of a Bible, an empty cross, an Orthodox icon and a lit candle – acts as a focus as the household prays together. But after the evening compline, enough futons are unfolded for the overnight guests. We ate our meals around a common table downstairs and only the leader has his own room, which by day serves as the front office for the household's many drop-in visitors. Theirs was a spirituality built coherently around a simplicity of household lifestyle, diet, hospitality and prayer. On each of the five nights I was there, different folks from the neighbourhood spontaneously joined us for the evening meal. There was bread for all. The hospitality shaped the community at prayer and at the meal table.

Pohl again: 'At the personal level, hospitality communicates to guests and strangers that they are valued: respect and recognition are expressed.'[3] If we as Christians are truly hospitable, we welcome both friend and stranger into our midst. We express that within our understanding of faith, our spirituality, guests are important not just to us but also to the God in whom we believe.

Coherent Christian spirituality cries for justice. Our Bibles contain over 1,060 references to '*justice*' although it is not always translated as such.[4] Whether it is within Anabaptist-Mennonite, Catholic Worker, Iona, Taizé or Waldensian 'circles', their spirituality cries in similar ways for justice. In each of their households, no one is left hungry for there is bread for all. As their emissaries, members and teachers go out from those households, they can do no more than repeat Jesus' kingdom's call for such justice and enough Jesus communities with tables where there will be bread for all.

So, how do you say grace before meals? Silently – to not embarrass your non-Christian guests? Or, one of the (grand-) children gabbles through the same hackneyed prayer? Or, the family joker proffers: 'Lord, bless these sinners as they eat their dinners?' Or, perhaps not at all? Or, with such a sense of thanksgiving for the food that we have and the guests sat with us, that unembarrassedly they feel welcomed into the presence and community of Jesus?

Feasting and fasting

Of course any cook will tell you it is easier to share a casserole meal – to be served with salad or vegetables, rice and/or homemade bread – with the unexpected guest rather than to divide up a set number of pork chops or chicken quarters. Galilean fishermen, like the first disciples, also knew about feast and famine, just as many Third World Christians do today. For me to share someone's hard-earned meal in a South American *favela*'s liberation community or a South African township is a sharp personal reminder of my western plenty.

'In offering hospitality, practitioners live between the vision of God's Kingdom in which there is enough, even abundance, and the hard realities of human life in which doors are closed and locked, and some needy people are turned away or left outside.'[5] It is the God-given responsibility of every First World (western) Christian to eat responsibly. Even in our hospitality and celebrations, the thought of excess must be tempered by the needs of those without. That will mean wrestling, like Stephen Webb, with whether we should be vegetarians, pescatarians or omnivores, whether on the grounds of animal welfare and/or planetary resources.[6]

Whatever the menu, Christians should learn to make people feel at home. That means serving good food but not in an excessive way. The Kreiders noted, 'Many outsiders find it easier to cross the threshold to a home church, where Jesus' presence is acknowledged in a meal.'[7] The quality, simplicity, consistency yet non-competitive style of meals on *Alpha* courses contribute to their success. Christians must learn that they need to make folk welcome, without having to 'blow the budget', for their pattern of hospitality to create community.

There is a place in the Christian community for both responsible daily eating and responsible celebrations involving food. British culture still marks Christmas Day as a feast day whereas the pattern of the big Easter Day lunch is diminishing rapidly for most. The loss of Easter as the high point of the Christian year is evidence of our post-Christendom culture. But there are many other occasions for community festivity.

But we do need to know the moments when to make something more of an occasion:

- Saying farewell to a family departing for Christian ministry elsewhere,
- Welcoming a new pastor or apostolic mission team,
- Leaving a now-redundant building,
- As a celebration for a piece of missional endeavour,
- At a 'barn-raising' – we do not all need to be Amish to realize that a shared piece of building work or renovation is more easily completed by the maxim: 'Many hands make light work.'

Sharing Food Builds Community – and is a Missional Resource

Food is both a missonal resource and a community-builder. But what will determine its effectiveness is the nature of our hospitality as Christians.

It is not just supper-parties-with-books that can be attractive to the non-believer. I have used Gabriel Axel's 1985 stark film, *Babette's Feast*, as well as Peter Weir's 1985 film, *Witness*, to begin discussions between believers and others about patterns of Christian hospitality as well as the 'feasting and fasting' issue.[8] Such groups can build friendships, while witnessing to our Jesus-based value system; over time, this creates relationships of sufficient strength in which questions of faith can be openly discussed.

But these are some way *before* individuals may be ready for the direct evangelistic approach of *Alpha* or a Jesus community's own version. The meal-sharing can make such a transition feel natural. In today's western and multi-media world, people are both inured and educated to believe there is no overarching story nor a single 'system' which provides the answers. Sociologists define this as a society without a great meta-narrative. This is evidence that we have entered an age defined as 'post-modernism'. Until individuals have sufficient and strong friendships with those who live out their belief in the Jesus meta-narrative, they will not be prepared to both engage with and give authority to that big story for themselves.

Our task is to remain faithful in our hospitality, witness and friendship-building. Let us not allow human impatience to coerce others towards discipleship programmes. It is God's mission – not ours. Theologians define this as the *missio Dei*, which simply means the 'mission of God'.[9]

The old sermons and revivalist hymns about God having no hands but ours seem to suggest that the task of hospitality is a very human way to participate in the *missio Dei*. Whether it is inviting the guys round to watch the ball game with a few beers, or a few neighbours to a summer barbecue, or starting a book group or whatever, this is all part of that *missio Dei*. So next Sunday, when the preacher demands, 'What are you doing for the mission of the church?', just remember first of all it is God's mission. Feel free to plan that occasion of Christian hospitality, as part of God's mission.

'The visibility of the church will not be the church's buildings but their common life, their service to their neighbors, and their collaboration in the *missio Dei*.'[10] Following Jesus is not isolationist – it calls us into new patterns of relationship with each other. We create community. One factor of radical Jesus communities is that they are *communities* – even if the house-sharing is limited to a few singletons in a shared house or Christian lodgers staying with families. The hospitality of such households, with everyone participating, acts as further witness to the nature of our Christian hospitality.

Shared households can testify to the power of Christian community. But so can the quality and frequency of friendships within a Jesus community. Excepting crises, Emmanuel URC had hardly anyone involved in house-sharing. It was their friendships, geographic proximity and frequent hospitality which exemplified a vital Jesus community – even though they did not practise purse-sharing, monastic vows and shared households. Their learning began with reading the gospels, following Jesus and then being open to what the *missio Dei* might mean if they opened their homes and shared their 'daily bread'.

In turn, how it affects our personal and communal spirituality will be determined by our openness to risk, offering hospitality, inviting others, building friendships. Then let God make this new community become Jesus-shaped – and that in turn will affect what we believe and what we pray (for)!

Part 2

Developing Practices: The Heat of the Kitchen

6

Building the New Community

Over the years of my adult life, I have encountered many different groups. Most of us recognize that as we mature we gravitate towards particular kinds of groups and experiences. After much searching, the pattern in my own life has increasingly found nurture, challenge and encouragement in small home-based groups. These groups seek to balance contemplation and activism, but all the time rooting these things in radical Christian faith.

I had learned that sharing my downtown terraced home with others was actually great fun, which easily outweighed the occasional problems. Lodgers came and went. But they began to stay longer, and become friends, as we built up a pattern of at least a couple of weekly communal meals. The kitchen and the table became central to a life together, as well as symbols of sharing work and hospitality for everyone. It was like a continuation of our respective student households – but this time without the squalor.

I recall the international college, where my parents worked during my early teenage years. Those who served at tables ate at those same tables too, with the students and the many invited guests, experiencing some sense of community. I remember my father rolling up his sleeves, operating the dishwasher, encouraging a high-ranking African government official to join the Sunday-evening student volunteer team of kitchen helpers. How much of that egalitarian spirit had been fostered in my grandparents' home, I will never know.

What I learned then, as well as those childhood episodes recounted at the beginning of the last chapter, set me on a lifetime's journey of sharing food, experiencing hospitality and discovering community.

Over my adult years, I have been helpfully nudged away from any Christendom leanings not just by radical Christians but also by liberation and feminist theologians. 'At the centre of Jesus' message, as prophet and wisdom teacher, is the vision of a world as an egalitarian community of beings, not a hierarchy of individuals.'[1] Sallie McFague helped give me the theological reasoning for what I knew instinctively in that lifetime journey from my grandparents' home.

The previous chapter's recounting of life and ministry within Emmanuel URC was but one stepping-stone on that journey. However, it was a big enough stepping-stone to attract the attention of my academic advisers in Princeton. It became the subject of a successful doctoral dissertation. Necessarily, this meant comparison between what I had previously experienced and others' practices, too. But even such study and research tended to push me back towards the model of Christendom – the congregation.

'Liberation theologies, on the other hand, have called for an awareness of social location in a much more radical sense.'[2] As a liberation theologian, Rieger invites Christians (and others) to think 'outside the box' of the church, in its institutional forms. We need to question and reflect upon our own experiences of Christian 'gathering' away from patterns driven by Sunday 'churchianity'. For this book's purpose, that 'gathering' must include those elements of welcome, hospitality and eating together.

Over those intervening adult years, I have experienced three other different but intertwined strands of developing practices. What is quickly apparent is that these are things that people have done and are doing. These are not pipe dreams shared conversationally over late-night coffee. I can offer them only as I have experienced them, so necessarily this chapter is autobiographical and anecdotal. But as I have previously shared these stories at conferences, in church weekends and short journal articles, others have found themselves not only saying, 'We should do that' but quickly getting on and doing so. So let me share these three different story-strands from my adult life.

The 'Pilgrim' Model

A few weeks earlier, I had been at a Christian CND rally. While walking back to the station, I met Maggie, whom I had known at school. Her partner, Max, had been in my school year, too. Together, we had been part of a crowd who went to Cornwall on holiday. Later, they both went to Hull University and spent their grants on buying one, then another terraced house which they let out to fellow-students.

'Look for the yellow house with a big fish in the window' was Max's instruction as I walked through east Hull, into their street. Theirs was the only sunshine-yellow painted door, with window-frames to match. There in the front bay window was a large painted papier-mâché fish. Over a meal, before my overnight ferry to Amsterdam, we shared a meal with their household. They were part of a network of four such local households – each had similar sunshine-yellow paintwork and papier-mâché fish in the front window.

Each household met together for their weekday evening meals. All four households took it in turn to host the weekly Sunday-evening meal for everyone. On Saturdays, the households ran a market stall, selling second-hand books, radical pamphlets and wholefoods. On Monday evenings, each household met for some quiet space around a lighted candle, having first discussed the Bible passage read to everyone the evening before. Over the ensuing months, they lent me radical books by those people known as Mennonites. One such book was John Howard Yoder's *The Politics of Jesus*,[3] of which I had encountered only a photocopied chapter before.

It was a long night on that ferry, as I reflected upon their vibrancy, comparing it to my then work as a minister in Liverpool. At least one of my congregations there simply wanted me to be chaplain to their kind of religious club. They were horrified when I took a former drug-addict in as a lodger, but I began to see and do other things. However, that reactionary congregation had helped fund the Rock Church Centre in Everton, where I went every Tuesday to the lunchtime service, eating afterwards with all who could stay. On Thursdays, some Christian friends, living on the Anfield Road, cooked for a group of unemployed men; I joined them for lunch and an afternoon of snooker in the basement.

Meanwhile, my smallest congregation in Woolton held a neighbourhood coffee morning each Saturday, selling home-made produce while others formed a work party. Amidst all this, ideas and vision germinated. Yoder's theology reminded me of college lectures about radical Anabaptist communities. I needed to know more.

Not just in my backyard

Gradually my visits to Hull became fewer. I learned of and visited other groups. I remember the striking clock, at the heart of a mid-Pennine town, punctuating the heavy silence of the quiet time of another local group.

I had been welcomed by them with hugs and a mug of coffee. Sitting at a trestle table, we ate a simple meal of bread and stew, before adjourning to a candle-lit first-floor lounge. There we sat on studio cushions or the floor. I had met our hosts, during a Christian conference, in a vegetarian café where the customers shared tables. Our ensuing conversation had brought this invitation.

Part of the evening was spent looking at their various photos of their group's August camping weekend, before several shared their stories for my benefit. They had all left the institutional church for varied, normally sad, reasons[4] and some had travelled nearly as far as I had (from Liverpool) for what was now identified as 'church' for them all. They met monthly, and for a New Year house-party and their summer camp. Yet several of them spoke of themselves as a 'community dispersed across many miles and households'. Years before, I had met with Iona Community members who had made similar comments about their members' regional group meeting. As that clock struck ten, we held hands and together said the Gaelic blessing, 'Deep peace of the running wave', before driving off into the night.

Even though my life was rooted in denominational Christianity, I was aware that many people were bravely making their spiritual journey outside the church. In every encounter with another group, communal sharing was deemed vital. Then almost every time, the idea of pilgrimage was openly identified. Folk saw their group not necessarily as the 'happy band of pilgrims' but as individuals whose common journeys brought them together as some form of provisional community.

Meanwhile, in Glasgow, a small group of justice-minded evangelicals began meeting for meals, Bible study and prayer, then flat-sharing. Their numbers grew, as did their commitment together, sharing resources, worship and homes. They worked with Iona Community activists campaigning for justice and for neighbourhood concerns. Several realized they were Anabaptists by nature, if not name. Nearly thirty years on, this small community called 'Bert' thrives, meeting weekly for a meal and their shared liturgy.

All these groups wanted to be 'something together' to disprove the attributed-to-Margaret-Thatcher notion that 'there is no such thing as community, just a set of individuals'. Time and again, I heard this desire for 'community' not only across Yorkshire and Scotland but elsewhere in similar home-based groups in Wales, the Pennines, East Anglia and Cornwall. Something was happening – and continues to do so.

The challenge to me to lead an inner-city ministry team took me to Leeds and another four-storey terraced home to share. To support each of the struggling participant congregations, we tried to develop communal households as well as congregational activities. Finally, five other local church leaders and I began meeting for prayer and a fortnightly meal. We became an activist group, challenging the injustices of the poll tax. Here was life beyond our own congregations. It began with hospitality and a desire to be community for each other.

Kent and beyond

That set a pattern, repeated with others, but most effectively in Kent nearly a decade later. My responsibility to train congregational lay leaders meant I quickly identified several couples and individuals who were isolated or working in tough situations. I sent around a flyer inviting them to commit to a fortnightly Friday evening meal, with prayer and discussion. All responded positively – we became lifelong friends. I had headed the flyer 'Pilgrim' and the name has stuck for us all.

This Kent Pilgrim group supported one member through the terminal illness of her husband. Another brought his new wife into the group. Three of the couples ended up moving to different villages in south-west France, where the whole group has met together again for holidays. Apart from the deep friendships, three constants remain:

- The joy of shared hospitality as we always shared a meal,
- A growing sense of God's hand guiding the group,
- The power of the communal prayer times.

The Pilgrim group have gone on to do other things as we all moved to live in different parts of southern England or France. Two of the France-based couples have begun separate new Pilgrim groups there while all of us in England have found ourselves within other small home-based Christian groups. Each of those subsequent groups shares a meal as well as their candid radical views before stilling their hearts in prayer.

As Nils-Arvid Bringéus, the Swedish ethnologist, notes, 'The dining table is the place where material, social and spiritual forces amalgamate.'[5] Whether in the Leeds group's challenge to the poll tax, the French group's commitment to eco-sustainability, Bert's neighbourhood commitment or my present group's development-aid campaigning, the conversation forged around tables leads to activism, theology and spirituality. The vitality and agenda created by such 'table churches' demonstrates Bringéus's conclusion. This was nowhere more apparent than in seeing each of those 'table churches' become committed to ensuring other members' well-being, materially as well as spiritually.

But the 'household'-rootedness of such initiatives should draw us back to bigger questions about mission. Meeks's statement, 'The centrality of the household has a further implication for the way we conceive of mission: it shows our modern, individualistic conceptions of evangelism and conversion to be quite inappropriate',[6] invites us to review our theological motivations. It also recognizes that membership of a group (however temporary) can speak more vibrantly of kingdom ways.

Café Church

Long before anyone had ever heard of *Alpha* or Willow Creek,[7] churches in these islands have been serving food. Church picnics, harvest suppers, Lent lunches and coffee mornings have all formed part of the diet of many UK congregations. As a visiting church leader, I was often given assurances about the quality of a congregation's food and hospitality even if they were totally uncertain about any quality guarantees of their mission.

Recently after a funeral in Leicester, without prompting, I heard two women discussing the low-key but joyfully offered hospitality of the nearby parish of St Peter's, Braunstone. Such examples communicate and create conversation about the Jesus-shaped community. 'Congregations committed to ministering to people in need sometimes overlook their greatest resource – the fellowship of believers.'[8] This was the very point made by the St Peter's vicar as I followed up that overheard conversation to verify the location.

From Bridlington to Brighton

For decades, churches have been running coffee mornings and hosting lunch clubs. Often, church members have failed to realize either their potential or the siting of many church buildings to use coherent hospitality in outreach.

In Armley, Leeds, we began a midweek Mums and Newborns Café, serving coffee and inexpensive nutritious home-cooked lunches, alongside bottle-warmers, a baby-clothes-exchange stall and free health leaflets. On the Penhill estate, the tiny URC started a monthly Saturday Caff selling bacon sandwiches, hot-dogs, home-made soup and cakes to increasing numbers. At Emmanuel URC, Haydon Wick, the monthly Saturday Good Earth Café serves great home-made cakes and lunches, alongside home produce, Fairtrade and second-hand book-exchange stalls.

In Ilkley, the large United Free Church went a step further, operating a six-day-per-week daytime café in its buildings next to the central shops and car park. In Swindon, the united Central Church's building was rebuilt incorporating a café and full professional kitchen, operated by trained volunteers all week. Similarly, on the Sussex coast, an Anglican church built a café annexe on its street frontage. In the Cotswolds, churches in Cirencester and Bourton-on-the-Water operate cafés in nearby shop-type premises

In Bridlington, Yorkshire, and Wells, Norfolk, Christian couples run commercial cafés, with help from family and paid staff from their local churches. These three different levels of 'operation' demonstrate how much Christians are recognizing that gathering places, hospitality and food are part of building relationships as a first step of sharing the gospel. They become the seedbed for developing Christian community.

Eucharist congregations

Sometime in the late 1970s, I was travelling through Sheffield with Christian acquaintances who decided we should call in on their friends at the Urban Theology Unit (UTU), mentioned in Chapter 2. I was fascinated by their communal households and variety of provisional congregations. I returned often.

A couple of years before that first visit, its director, John Vincent, and some other friends began the 'Eucharist Congregation', meeting over Sunday lunchtime in a town-centre restaurant. Radical politics, God-talk and Holy Communion formed the agenda and forged many human friendships. To ease the costs for all, the venue quickly moved to UTU's study house in Pitsmoor. Within a decade, this single Eucharist Congregation had spawned several other activities, including midweek home-based meal groups, a Friday-evening teenagers' group and an all-age drama group. Many single people were drawn into active faith through all these and by the early 1980s a sufficient number joined together to form an independent liberation congregation. None of these things are still in the same shape in the twenty-first century – and rightly so.

Outside of student neighbourhoods and 'bedsitland', I struggled to replicate lunchtime Eucharist congregations; perhaps a surplus of single folk was necessary. While in Liverpool, frustrated by over-formal Presbyterian quarterly Communions, I introduced another six short, informal breakfast Communions each year, marking the onset of Advent and Lent, etc.

In suburban Leeds, we took this idea further, developing monthly 9.00 a.m. Communions, followed by a simple breakfast of coffee, orange juice and hot rolls; toasters quickly arrived too, as the breakfasts and numbers attending grew. I learned from that and introduced the pattern in Kent, first to a Sevenoaks congregation, then elsewhere. In each congregation, these Communion services with their breakfasts afterwards have remained, often developing as specific eucharistic congregations – echoing their 8.00 a.m. counterparts in many Anglican churches.

Willow Creek, Alpha *and more*

In the 1980s, several of my colleagues crossed the Atlantic to visit Willow Creek, where Bill Hybels and his team had developed weekly worship built around a café-cabaret format, requiring little participation by the audience-congregation. There was a lot to be learned. Now some UK 'alternative worship' practitioners are benefiting from those lessons. It has been much harder to persuade traditional congregations to worship comfortably while sitting round café tables to welcome non-believers and other visitors.

'Café church' works. An Anglican church close to the main hospital in Bath attracts shift workers in; they know they can leave without feeling uncomfortable. Barney Barron tells the story of the Warren Park Café Church which he leads on a Havant estate where a double booking meant they had to use the community centre's café for meeting – the congregation felt so at home they decided to continue to meet there on Friday evenings. For several years, a pub-based group in south London, known as 'Holy Joe's', operated a café-style format for meeting.

At Emmanuel, the elders came up with their own variation called 'Scones of Praise'. Building upon the older generation's recognition of BBC TV's *Songs of Praise*, tea tables were set out in the church orchard on well-publicized summer Sunday afternoons. Attendances were beyond expectations as popular hymns were sung with regular breaks for scones, jam and cream teas. Now a neighbouring Baptist congregation has also joined in with a monthly Sunday-afternoon tea-with-hymns.

Far more UK congregations have had experience of the *Alpha* course with its meal-song-talk-discussion format; reference has been made to *Alpha* in earlier chapters. For many churches, it has been an unfamiliar process to regularly welcome non-churchgoers to eat in their midst. While *Alpha* has its detractors, a major contributory factor to its success seems to be the shared meal – particularly in those communities with much social isolation or high numbers of single-person households.

My west Kent congregations proved to be almost perfect at adopting the *Alpha* format and ethos. Newcomers came into the church, and some into faith, because of the hospitality given. Yet many did not stay because the elders could not persuade nor adapt the whole congregational programme to have the same hospitality and patterns of shared meals. I learned a hard lesson about the necessity of consistency in what we do as Christian communities.

My perception is that more congregations are prepared to openly try café-style worship on particular Sundays or other occasions when many visitors have been invited after a 'publicity push'. The above comment about consistency should have clear application here. How much can those who encounter the congregation in 'café church' be expected to transition to 'normal Sunday worship'? Perhaps 'inherited churches' need to support more initiatives like Holy Joe's (the open congregation that gathered in a south London pub) or the Bible study which I led every week over eighteen months in an inner-city Leeds pub to create a more authentic point of contact.

I remain convinced that a 'meals strategy', prayerfully planned throughout a local congregation, may prove to be the more effective long-term way for them to build local contacts. 'During the course of the meal, each person has to have the chance to meet all the others. Even the simple gesture of passing the potatoes is a natural moment of communication which can bring people out of their isolation. They cannot remain behind the barriers of their depression when they have to ask for the salt. The need for food encourages communication.'[9] Jean Vanier's life-experience in the therapeutic L'Arche Communities has much to teach us; the table may be the place where community can begin, whether in a café or a home.

The Church Comes Home

As I left Liverpool in 1987, a house-church leader gave me a book entitled *The Church Comes Home* by Robert Banks, then a

Californian academic.[10] Banks described how there and in his native Australia he had formed a series of home-based churches. Each of these had its own life and vibrancy. It was exciting to find a thesis which drew together several strands of both my life and theological reflection.

House churches

Even during my sixth-form days, I was conscious that some of my peers were leaving their parents' churches. They were joining groups of Christians, normally meeting in someone's front room. My then radical faith and political views meant I was more sceptical of these groups' evangelistic questions ('When were you saved?') and charismatic practices than their longer-term survival.

As my faith matured, my scepticism diminished. Several of these groups grew significantly. They joined other front-room groups and became independent churches. As my contacts with such groups grew, I observed two things.

1 They had been attractive to those who felt disenfranchised by traditional, denominational Christianity.
2 Very few seemed to have made hospitality beyond coffee and biscuits central to their then pattern of welcome.

Rightly, the term the 'New Church Movement' should be applied to this vital strand of Christianity, rather than the term 'House Church'. I had a pleasant surprise, revisiting a chapel I had known in its damp darkness as a child. It had been bought by one such New Church and was now warm, carpeted and well-lit with its new PA system assisting worship. Regrettably, they did admit they hardly ever used their beautifully refurbished kitchen.

Reflecting back, I realized it was nearly always those home-based groups that became the New Churches. They avoided the use of the concept or word 'pilgrim' and used shared meals, such as barbecues, only in mission contexts. They may have been pioneers but perhaps their intention was always to become settlers, with buildings and programmes, rather than pilgrims forever.

Interestingly, as many New Churches come up to their second generation, I am increasingly approached by their leaders to share my findings upon hospitality, community and mission. Perhaps, as they become established, even the New Churches must rediscover ways of not appearing to offer the same traditional things as the more historic church down the road. Stuart Murray, an incisive church consultant, observes this too: 'What appeared cutting edge in the 1970s looked decidedly passé by the 1990s. The pioneers' children decamped and searched for alternative expressions of church.'[11]

My message is simple. Folk always have to eat and very few shun the opportunity to share a well-cooked and presented meal – particularly if the hospitality is offered within a genuine community. Alan and Eleanor Kreider, the often-quoted world-renowned Christian educators, frequently make this point: 'The Christians' hospitality to the outsider grows out of the Christian culture that has shaped them, in which they have welcomed each other' in post-Christendom.[12] Patchway Baptist Church demonstrates such an ethos as their welcome pack includes a standing invitation to dinner.

Activist cells

In marked counterpoint to the 'home-group plus home-group' development pattern of many of the New Churches, there are those activist cells that have taken a different path. This is evidenced earlier in this chapter by the east Hull 'Yellow Doors' or Glasgow's 'Bert' community and Sheffield's Eucharist Congregation, as well as some of the Pilgrim groups.

Here in Wiltshire, I know a home-based group which grew out of their local Amnesty International group. They now own a van, which different folk take to weekly markets with home-baked bread and other produce, from their kitchens and allotments, as well as books and petitions. The money raised goes to Third World development charities. Apart from their Wednesday and Sunday gatherings, the only visible sign of their faith is a carved wooden fish next to the wind-chimes on their stall. As in east Hull, the fish as a symbol of the acrostic 'Jesus Christ – God's Son – Saviour' is used to show their 'sense of community rather than the cross as a sign of more individualistic faith'; that is how they describe it.

While spending some weeks at Ruskin Trade Union College, Oxford, I linked up for a couple of evening meals with a then similar local group who came together around peace-making issues. Several of its women became involved at Greenham Common.[13] They wrote letters, organized petitions and coaches to rallies, meeting together over food every fortnight, before discussing some more of Jesus' words.

Years ago, I spent a weekend in Hulme, Manchester, working as a volunteer with another local group. We were the muscle to help build an adventure playground on wasteland. This was long before Health and Safety legislation would have stopped us. We barbecued sausages on the Saturday-night bonfire of our scrap lumber; the resulting hot-dogs were given to local residents' children who would become the playground's users. We worked hard, ate well, drank cheap beer and spent the evenings singing and reading back copies of the *Catonsville Roadrunner* (that underground Christian magazine, which one of the group had helped to edit!). But as with all these activist cells, it was the eating together and the hospitality to newcomers and residents which welded us together as a group.

Being flexible

I was much happier when a second and revised edition of Banks's *The Church Comes Home*[14] appeared in 1994. The new edition still expressed the vibrancy of the home-church concept but spoke much more coherently about the potential for flexibility.

People's lives change; they have children, some get married, redundancy and serious illness occurs, divorce can happen. Groups which have met frequently can be very challenged by life-changes; some cope but not all groups survive. Equally, some groups come together around a particular issue or need, such as the poll tax or local educational policies; when they have done their work they end and people move on.

Banks's thesis is that such home-based, emerging churches are effectively 'community'. This is underlined by the nature of the UK emerging church movement in this 2010+ decade. 'There are many Christians who are longing for what can be found in a home church . . . They ache to belong to a genuinely compassionate and relevant community.'[15]

Banks is clear that groups must remain flexible. Whether they occasionally work with or even regularly meet other like-minded groups must remain an option. So is the need to change direction and style, as participants and their needs change and grow. What is at the heart of Banks's thesis is that each home-based group creates the space to meet-and-eat, to undertake some appropriate level of Christian study, often to pray but always to exercise a care for each other. That sounds like a very New Testament pattern. It seems no surprise that participants in such groups have left behind traditional-denominational 'Sunday-best Christianity'. These are localized forms of 'dispersed community'.

Apart from my local contacts and those mentioned already, I know of other such groups in Cambridge, the north-east and the West Midlands. Each of these groups retains that sense of flexibility but all have different emphases. What gives them similarity is fourfold:

- They are home-based groups,
- They eat regularly together, sharing that hospitality,
- They perceive themselves as some kind of community or extended family,
- They are all rooted in a vibrant faith that acknowledges Jesus as the exemplar for discipleship.

At a recent theological forum, I heard the leader of another ongoing group, the Sanctuary in Billingham, delineate those same four key principles. The Sanctuary has drawn together a regular Saturday-evening, home-based 'table fellowship'. He was adamant that the talk about Jesus' ways was vital to the group if it was to have any longer-term purpose to the wider life of the local town's Christian community. This is such a refreshing New Testament perspective.

However, Christians need to be explicit about who Jesus is for them. There are those humanists who see Jesus in a similar way to Mahatma Gandhi as exemplars for living – but they reject the theological claims and spiritual relationships which Christians have. So Christians, in such small groups, need to:

- Be explicit that Jesus is Lord and not just a 'jolly good man',
- Acknowledge their struggles with praying, and

- Show that the biblical testimony of Jesus as Saviour of the world (John 3:16–17) is true.

The Journey Continues

This chapter's sections are three predominantly autobiographical strands. Alongside Emmanuel URC (in Chapter 3), they provide concrete examples of developing practices of hospitality and community in differing ways, gathered over thirty-plus years. They are not simply discussion options at a mission conference. For most, the journey continues.

Today, the Hull houses with the yellow doors and the big fish in the windows are gone – sold. Our lives evolve. If we are not to ossify, our faith communities need to evolve too. For some, the heat in their kitchen becomes too much. For others, the heat cooks up something new and different. Each narrative strand's example has been worked out 'on the hoof' – as their journeys progressed. My life and many others were changed by the community behind those yellow doors. But every meal and each encounter with each of these faith initiatives was life-changing.

The diversity of all these activities, communities and projects emphasized principles which I had first seen and heard about during teenage visits to the Taizé and Iona communities. I recognize that discipleship is teaching similar lessons across Britain, to those previously declared in rural Burgundy and Hebridean Iona as well as in the New Testament and radical church history.

I have been privileged to hear the founding prior of Taizé, Brother Roger, teach that today's church must always respect the 'dynamic of the provisional'; he later used this as the title of some of his diary entries. With equal clarity, I have heard the modern Iona Community's founder, the Revd Dr George McLeod, preach about discovering new ways of living Jesus' ministry now – without being tied to the institutional church. Both these visionary men came from orthodox Reformed churches yet spoke with the prophetic voice of the Radical Reformers.

In developing home-based churches, Banks identified 'four factors that are an integral part of a new home church: a solid foundation, a basic commitment, a framework of belief and a pastoral centre'.[16] The experience of the UK emerging churches now, as they are beginning to establish themselves, all have the four factors; whether they openly declare them or identify them similarly is irrelevant. All the Pilgrim groups, which I started or have had an involvement with, also had those same four factors. The development of the Ashram, Iona and Taizé communities during the second half of last century shared those four principles. They are essential to other communities – dispersed or residential – too.

Pressures and stresses do arise. How we meet them and/or deal with them will determine the survival and growth of whatever group, home church or community we are part of. Crises occur – whether in human relationships or from external factors. Bonhoeffer wrote, 'A community which cannot bear and cannot survive such a crisis, which insists upon keeping its illusion when it should be shattered, permanently loses in that moment the promise of Christian community.'[17] Just as we are prepared to plant, we must be prepared to let failing initiatives die.

'True community only develops *as we learn to face the reality of our differences and work through them together . . .* The chief hindrances to our becoming a genuine Christian community lie within us: in our basic attitudes, expectations and motives'[18] (my italics). The key personal questions are:

1 How much do I expect to change to be part of the new community?
2 Once I am together with others in a new venture, how much change can our group manage to cope with?

Each of these developing ecclesial practices, described above, has its human costs. For the majority, this has been to leave the security of 'doing what we've always done'. As with any gift of hospitality, another meal has to be cooked so the heat of the kitchen is constantly there. That is not just the literal heat of literal kitchens, it is also the heat of the emotional kitchen. These are where the recipe and ingredients for God's new community come together, knowing that tomorrow it may all have to change again. And probably will.

7

What Kind of 'Community' Do People Want?

Post-Christendom is marked by a renewed interest in spirituality. For some the outworking of this may result in interest in New Age practices, or esotericism, or paganism, or eastern-based religions such as Buddhism. The late twentieth and early twenty-first centuries are marked by people's right to choose to believe what is most appropriate for their circumstance. It is quite common to encounter those with a 'pick-and-mix' spirituality, drawing on several diverse sources.

As already stated, the educational and media worlds no longer sustain any particular overarching grand theory (or meta-narrative). This is at least from a faith perspective. There is a popular, secular humanism pervading western society, supported by a scientific world-view. The events of 9/11 and the recent world recession may lead thinking people to question where that secularist view, accompanied by seeming ongoing materialism, is leading us. Only now are the post-war baby-boomers realizing that their own children cannot, and will not, accrue similar wealth as they did nor be able to use earth's resources as they have.

The philosophy of 'more' is coming to its end. The failing economy will see to that. When asked what people want, contemporary answers tend toward the emotional and philosophical (e.g. 'wanting contentment') rather than the acquisitional. In my encounters with recently bereaved baby-boomer families, questions of spirituality do arise but decreasingly are such people looking to Christendom-style certainties for help and resource.

As an occasional celebrant at an eco-burial woodland, I far more encounter that pick-and-mix spirituality, rather than a seemingly distant Christianity.

The Christendom church has found itself under the microscope of media scrutiny and popular ridicule. As its positive qualities have been ignored, historic denominational Christianity has been found wanting in the eyes of the masses. The autumn 2011 debacle and seeming infighting of the St Paul's Cathedral clergy, as 'Occupy London' was on its doorstep, is symptomatic of historic Christianity's failings to many.

The UK is now a country where more Muslims are in mosques on Fridays than Anglicans are in church on Sundays. Weekly churchgoing is now a habit of less than 5 per cent of the population. Sunday church attendance is not what people want.

For some young white British citizens, the past decadence, seeming hypocrisy and the church's complicity with a materialist state drives them towards conversion to Islam, with its clear and rigorous demands. When the sons or daughters of UK cabinet ministers and English titled families as well as those of Middle England take much-publicized similar steps into Islam, the time has come for some to ask, again, searching questions of the Christendom church. Is its mission is still Jesus-shaped? One worrying fact of such questioning is that it often becomes both right-wing and individualistic. This creates a negative tendency to consider these converts and the peace-loving Muslim majority as sharing a common mindset with 9/11's perpetrators and jihadists.

Learning from the Models of the Past

The post-Christendom church must be careful not to throw the baby out with the bathwater. Not everything from our (UK) Christian heritage was bad but not all of it can be for our good – now. There are things which we cannot change, such as the canon of the Bible.[1] But within the life and practice of the Jesus-shaped church, we can choose to respond to the changing circumstances of the post-Christendom landscape.

Cathedral-style worship

Most English cathedrals are reporting steadily growing congregations. It is far too soon, with too little documentary evidence, to fully understand this or accept it *will* be a long-term trend, but it must be noted. Obviously both the setting and significant numbers provide space for a rich, traditional liturgy – often accompanied by well-schooled choirs, brass instruments and a good organist – to create powerful, often exemplary (of its type) worship experiences.

Interestingly, in many of the tourist cities or the cathedrals' own refectories, one can find small groups of cathedral worshippers beginning to meet together for coffee and/or lunch after Sunday worship. This suggests that worship-based relationships are being forged. For the longer term, this invites questions and research about the potential development of the dispersed cathedral community. But when meeting these small groups, one notices other individuals or couples who anonymously arrive and depart without actively engaging with their fellow-worshippers – theirs is spirituality without community. For these latter individuals, anecdotal evidence suggests that it is both the anonymity and lack of demanded involvement which makes cathedral-style worship attractive.

But within Anglicanism, it is possible to step down an ecclesial tier and discover similar worshipper-responses in minster congregations such as at Beverley, Yorkshire, and York, or the abbey congregations in Bath and Tewkesbury. Historically of course, both abbeys and minsters were Christian centres, often monastic, of worship, learning and mission, sending out clergy and teachers to work in not-so-local neighbourhoods. Interestingly both the English Roman Catholic hierarchy and some historic Free Church denominations are looking at patterns of ecclesial consolidation to create 'minster' models of mission and ministry.[2]

Historic spirituality

What is exciting is that many of these traditional liturgical resources are being adopted within many of the emerging churches. In the 'alternative worship' movement, the use of traditional church buildings and choral, ambient or Taizé music or prayer stations (with icons, candles, crosses) or practices like prayer labyrinths are speaking to many dechurched, even unchurched students, as well as those in their twenties and thirties. Often the fact that such times of alternative worship have a café or running buffet alongside them, thus extending hospitality, is noteworthy. These, often monthly, events are normally planned over a meal table by a small group, creating a sense of a core community.

More will be said about emerging churches below and in the next chapter; but regrettably not all the different variants can be surveyed. Another popular variant is that of the 'boiler room', in which 24/7 prayer is practised overnight or for a weekend. Often – but not always – this draws on a pattern of 'offices', modelled on the sevenfold pattern of daily prayer of monasteries and past cathedral communities. Perhaps surprisingly, the Salvation Army along with both Free and New Church groups have been at the forefront of such 24/7 initiatives, which draw on these historic traditions of prayer. E-mails on my computer tell of 'boiler rooms' from Southampton to Scotland, built around a temporary dormitory and 24/7 kitchen to provide both hospitality and a sense of community to participants.

A time for dialogue?

In sharp contrast, the great 'preaching churches' of past years are not attracting folk in their droves to listen to sermons. If the snapshot is taken at successive (approximate generational) 25-year intervals from the late nineteenth century, numbers have fallen. Whether one considers the self-reported figures of Carrs Lane Church, Birmingham; St Giles in Edinburgh; Wesley's Chapel or the City Temple, both in London; this pattern is replicated.

Our media has created a world of soundbite politics. This makes the tasks of serious listening, polished delivery or academic lecture become alien phenomena. Sermons are not academic lectures. If they were, it would be hardly surprising that people did not want them. Today, people are not wanting, nor are they able to listen at length – and this is not just to sermons. Even university undergraduates straight from schools, full of interactive educational methods and multi-media, struggle with hour-long lectures.

The age of the great preachers, like Leslie Weatherhead, Donald Soper and George MacLeod, may well be past. Certainly the civic and social influences upon the literal thousands who listened to both the Congregationalist, R.W. Dale, or the Baptist, Charles Haddon Spurgeon, in the nineteenth century are over. Churches are and have to keep reinventing their mode of communication.

Anglican and Roman Catholic clergy, used to delivering short, cogent homilies, are at an advantage over Free Church ministers who were schooled in the doctrinaire, alliterative, three-point 20-minute-plus sermon.[3] It may say a lot that the half-hour talks of each *Alpha* course session are preceded by a meal, with conversation and humour, rather than some traditional hymns, prayers and unfamiliar chunks of the Bible. The forthcoming companion volume to this, *Preaching After Christendom*,[4] by Glen Marshall, highlights many of the questions which the Christendom church have failed to address in their underlying assumptions.

Having said all this, people do and will still go to neighbourhood or parish-level congregations, because they are distinctive or meet their personal need. I have many friends who remain in inherited denominational congregations. Structured conversations with over twenty friends (all in leadership positions) while researching this book, revealed three common reasons:

- They still believed that highly visible Christian congregations *need* to exist, with identifiable buildings and patterns of mission-oriented activity.
- They believed that for them as twenty- to fifty-somethings, to simply abandon such traditionalist congregations would make those churches lose viability, with no guarantee that the potential alternatives either could or can exercise more effective mission.
- They believe that new patterns of hospitality and welcome will emerge, enabling a different pattern of 'shared life' from 'simply Sunday worship' (no one baulked when I suggested this new pattern could be called 'community').

It is vital that all Christians keep talking with one another, respecting each other's patterns of mission. But this must not become like the late twentieth century when talks about sharing ecumenically so predominated that coherent prayer-sharing or mission strategy appeared to be excluded. Equally, Christians must avoid polarizing and pigeonholing others in our common search towards renewed and relevant mission.

Increasingly, without significant mission, the age profile or lack of numbers attending, or dry rot or urban redevelopment will mean that more traditional church buildings become non-viable and those congregations will close. But while faith in Jesus' grace and his kingdom's imperatives continue, Christians will gather in what many of those participants call 'churches', whether or not they regard hospitality as vital or perceive themselves as 'Jesus communities'. Until they see, accept and learn about alternatives, the habits of their past will be, for some, regarded as the *only* key to survival.

Even that word 'traditional' must be questioned; I know many New Churches who talk of 'their tradition'. Stuart Murray has helpfully encouraged the discussion about what language and terms we should use. To use 'inherited church' is less value-laden than alternatives like 'traditional', 'established' or 'mainstream'. 'The use of "emerging church" is intended to preclude both judgmental attitudes towards "inherited churches" and over-optimistic assessments to what has not yet emerged.'[5]

Dispersed Communities and Emerging Churches

Post-Christendom is marked not only by a resurgence of interest in spirituality, but also by renewed interest in patterns of community. This may be driven by social isolation, marginalization and urban growth. My experience tells me that more folk are interested in having close-bonded, non-familial significant relationships with a few others than at any time since the 1960s hippy movements. The patterns and examples offered in the previous chapters exemplify this.

After the Second World War, the Taizé Community began hosting week-long summer camps for young people from across Europe. To share in the daily worship and communal meals provides an experience of welcome, hospitality and community. For several years I used to take an annual summer student-age group to share this Taizé experience. Other faces became familiar as I recognized them making one of their annual pilgrimages there. Several admitted that they were part of Taizé cells back at home rather than traditional congregations. Despite their widespread dispersion, they were informally making themselves part of an extended Taizé community. Some of the current professed Taizé Brothers began their contacts as such summer campers, later formalizing that commitment in lifetime vows.

Not only in the British Isles, but globally, the Iona Community has chosen to encourage and nurture a similar sense of dispersed community. Those who are full members make an annual five-fold recommitment to the community,[6] including to daily prayer and Bible study, peace and justice activism and an economic discipline. Another commitment is to meet regularly and regionally with those associate members who make similar but less stringent commitments; this pattern was referred to in Chapter 2. There is also a wider circle of friends, committed to prayer and support of the community and its mission.

Membership and mother houses[7]

These concentric patterns of commitment are echoed too in the lives of newer 'dispersed communities' such as the Ashram Community, the Anabaptist Network and the Northumbria Community. Each respectively have their mother houses in Sheffield's Urban Theology Unit, the national Mennonite Centre (in Selly Oak, Birmingham) and Acton Home Farm (Felton, Northumberland). Each serves as a welcoming centre of 'hospitality, resource, learning and vision' for their respective constituencies. The latter two have recently moved, demonstrating that geography is less important than the relationships created between their collaborative leadership, their core steering groups, their regional study and prayer groups and their wider membership – all fostered by the hospitality shared with each other.

Each of these three groups (along with many others) will acknowledge their debt of learning from the Iona and Taizé experiences. Iona, by developing intention, used the historic Iona Abbey as a 'mother house'. By default, that Cluniac village and expanding summer camp have effectively become the 'mother house' for the global Taizé movement. Again, it is too early to say definitively and there is little documentary evidence, but patterns of 'dispersed community' seem to be part of the answer to: What do people want? The 'street cred' of Taizé, Iona, Ashram, Northumbria and the Anabaptist movement in reaching beyond dechurched Christians is growing. This suggests that their patterns of hospitality and dispersed community are missional.

New monasticism

There is a growing interest in what is called the 'new monasticism'. The Anabaptist Network and Northumbria Community have held a series of well-attended day conferences on this subject, which has also been part of the Spring Harvest agenda. One strand of interest is in the models of worship or patterns of published daily offices which individuals, couples and small groups use domestically. Both the Anabaptists[8] and the Northumbria Community[9] have such resources available. Long before writing this volume, I became aware of small 'pockets' of folk who meet once or twice per week in one of their homes to share together in one of these published offices, either meeting for breakfast afterwards or supper beforehand. The obvious hospitality involved has led such little groups in Dorset and East Anglia to write, describing themselves as creating 'a sense of community'. Another similar office-based pocket of folk in Derbyshire were all dechurched but now meet in a similar weekly way with a meal.

The other predominant strand of interest is the communal expression of 'new monasticism'. In various sometimes haphazard ways, individuals have begun using a mother house for a monthly communal weekend of prayer and study; some have also included overnight silence or communal craft as part of their weekend's rhythm. For many years, small groups of Christians have set themselves up in various patterns of long-term community[10] but without the professed vows of the historic monastic communities. These newer groups differ in that theirs is a periodic communal experience.

I first encountered this in the 1990s with the extended or dispersed Omega Community at one of their communal weekends at their Chew Magna mother house, which supported itself as a retreat and conference centre between its specifically Omega Community monthly weekends and twice-yearly week-long retreats for its own members, who followed patterns of individual contemplation when back at home.

Another challenging development has been the re-invention of residential 'intentional community'. The work of new religious communities, meeting particular therapeutically social and/or spiritual needs, deserves monitoring. Houses such as the Well at Willen, near Milton Keynes, or the two Pilsden Communities, in Kent and Dorset, exemplify this development. Their respective ministries have become encouraging 'wells of spirituality' for local Christians.

Emerging churches

Reference has already been made to the 'emerging church movement'. Defining this is as hard as defining post-Christendom, because each expression is part of a multifaceted spectrum. Some are larger, such as those putting on 'alternative worship' events. Noting already that many of these are planned by a core group, meeting over a meal or two, invites a question about what kind of community they *may* be becoming. Others are much smaller, tending to be home-based; very naturally, food and hospitality form part of their agenda. It is far easier to invite local acquaintances for a meal than for a Bible study, for as relationships strengthen, friendships are formed, witness continues and Christian cells come into being. Alan and Eleanor Kreider make this very point: 'many outsiders find it easier to cross the threshold to a home church, where Jesus' presence is acknowledged in a meal . . . than it is to enter a church building for a gathering of a Christian congregation'.[11]

Emerging churches often begin life as both home-based and homogeneous Christian cells but with the potential to reach out beyond themselves and grow. 'Home churches, often called table churches, are a contemporary analogue to the house churches of the New Testament. Patterns of life and worship that Paul describes in 1 Corinthians were culturally appropriate in pre-Christendom; and they are once again emerging as Christendom wanes.'[12]

In today's world of recession and social fragmentation, one answer to 'What do people want?' is candour in their friends and neighbours; Jesus-shaped discipleship is honest and hospitable.

A Post-Christendom Landscape

This book has no brief to present some future apocalyptic scenario. However, we need to be aware of potential trouble ahead.

Social changes happen

In reviewing the New Testament churches' locations, one realizes that the landscapes of the majority of them are now entirely different. Even if these churches were city-wide networks of home churches, they were sufficiently known to attract apostolic attention, letters, rebuke and encouragement. How many of the Pauline churches still proliferate? How many of the locations of Revelation's seven churches, in chapters 2 and 3, are still home to vibrant Christian communities? Very few – times and circumstances change.

In the days of the pre-Christendom church, areas like north Africa were Christian strongholds, nurturing many, including the renowned theologian, Augustine of Hippo. Similarly, in the Middle East, the Christian communities of Syria, Persia and other countries were equally strongholds of vibrant discipleship. These regions are now regarded as Muslim. Indeed, quality western media often report the current persecution of Christians in these areas.[13] Times and circumstances change.

Who in Christendom could have imagined the general acceptance of the barbed humour now levied by household-name comedians against the church? The cynical antagonism towards Christian faith in some broadcast programmes at Christmas or Easter tells of the marginalization of the church. Who in Christendom would have expected to hear French newsreaders questioning whether France is 'really a Catholic country anymore'? Times and circumstances change.

There is much anecdotal evidence as well as research – both of which have been referred to at various points in this *After Christendom* series – highlighting the demise of institutional Christianity in the UK. While senior Anglican clergy still officiate at royal weddings or have involvement in the coronation in Westminster Abbey, many outside the church will assume all is well and the Christian church will 'be there'. Those inside the church know that *may* be false.

But most of those who have no active involvement in Christian activity still consider the church an anachronism for everyday living. Unlike radical Christians who favour rejecting the church-state complicity of Christendom, the vast British majority seems to favour some form of transmutation, only taking the church out of its box when it needs to be centre stage, for events like the wedding of Prince William to Catherine Middleton.

Making a difference

So the Christian church needs to face up to the challenges and respond creatively. Those who follow the way of Jesus will need to demonstrate, in their daily living, that the teaching and example of Jesus make a qualitative difference to life. Then their friends and neighbours will want to find out more.

Christians and other churchgoers will need to hear the less palatable things from church or mission audits, then act upon them. I was involved in such an audit and had to take several disbelieving church members to meet one of our nearest shopkeepers, who knew nothing of our church or even the existence of its buildings only 500 metres away.

In the 1990s, my consultancy with another congregation persuaded them to host a lunch for the local GPs, town councillors and the two local primary-school head teachers. The majority of these guests were honest enough to say they knew nothing of that congregation's daily preschool playgroup, twice-weekly pensioners' lunch club nor most other activities, even though all those lunching lived or worked within one kilometre. Churches need to face up to the fact that their expectations of communication, by osmosis or whatever, no longer materialize.

In the UK Coalition Government's 2011 call to return to 'the Big Society', most politicians did not see nor acknowledge the churches' potential involvement in that. Yet at the start of the twenty-first century, the UK's Christian churches were the biggest providers of volunteer-run community activities. It was left to the leaders of inherited churches, both locally and nationally, to

encourage both those politicians and their attendant media to realize that the 'Big Society' demand (however laudable or question-
able) had and has implications far beyond a single parliamentary
term.

Key questions remain in that 'Big Society politik' as to whether
it will cause or force the churches to become serious domestic
providers of social aid or health care as in the Victorian and
medieval eras. Already churches running day centres – whether
for the elderly, unemployed or psychiatrically fragile – are having
to look to raise their own financial backing rather than receive
grant-aid from or via the local authority to run such services.
However, critics can fairly argue that this is simply a transmutation of the Christendom model as the church is choosing to act
compliantly with the state. The radical alternative is to also
prophetically remind the state of its social responsibilities.

A church for the people

Whatever the outcome of that argument, such social care often
naturally involves hospitality, be that in the free or subsidized
provision of at least light refreshments if not meals. For many of
the socially isolated – including being a single-parent, elderly,
unemployed or mentally fragile – eating together in such church-
based centres is life-giving. It may be one of the few occasions on
which they experience any sense of adult family or human
community. As in the days of the New Testament church, post-
Christendom Christians may find their 'life together' and witness
speaks to those who are marginalized rather than to the rich and
powerful, who still need to hear Jesus' comments about the eye
of a needle.

The gospel calls people into community, not isolation; whereas
western societal pressures do the reverse. In this upside-down
kingdom of Jesus, Donald Kraybill reminds us: 'Jubilee giving
assumes that one form of giving is not to take money from others
in the first place.'[14] A key issue for the post-Christendom church
will be to stop asking for money to maintain inappropriate and
large buildings for worship. Unless a church's building is daily
serving the real needs of its neighbourhood, it is obsolete.
Christians increasingly need to question how much it costs to
maintain church buildings and then revisit Jesus' advocacy in

Matthew 19:24. Jesus-shaped discipleship in post-Christendom will require radical thinking.

'Various contemporary observers predict that worship in houses, as in the early church, will be the normal experience of a growing number of Christians after Christendom.'[15] 'Table churches', 'emerging churches', Christian 'cells' and 'pockets' tell of this growing trend. This will demand fresh thinking about resources and leadership; we return to these themes in the next chapter.

The Jesus Challenge

Whether it is eastern religion, esotericism or pick-and-mix spirituality, people accept difficult practices or demands, discipline and sacrifice, in order to achieve the faith they want. Westerners converting to Islam learn Arabic, practise alms-giving, read the Koran, and adopt fivefold practices of daily prayer and simplicity of life to follow the faith they want. Those who are truly interested in vital, life-enriching faith will change their lifestyles, setting aside past priorities.

The Christendom church has done little for the kingdom of God in its acceptance of mere Sunday 'churchianity' or a lowest-common-denominator membership and a diluted theism which ignores much of Jesus' radical teaching.

In the companion volume to this, *Reading the Bible After Christendom*, Lloyd Pieterson makes Jesus' challenge explicit in reviewing the gospels. 'Mark makes it clear that Jesus is hard to understand and tough to follow!'[16] 'Luke, emphasizing the role of the Spirit, the good news for the poor, the notion of eschatological reversal which figures strongly in the Magnificat, and the introduction of Jubilee themes from Leviticus 25 . . . remission of debts . . . redistribution of capital wealth. This liberating good news is too radical for many.'[17] Yet this is the way of Jesus, which I was nurtured within in Anabaptist congregations. Many others have become equally committed to such radical streams of Christianity.

Sadly much of the Christendom church, over its centuries, has ignored or diluted the radical nature of Jesus. Worse still, it has corrupted that 'good news' in the aggrandisement of clergy, its support for state-sanctioned violence (e.g. warfare, capital punishment) and the accumulation of wealth and resources, while the poor starve and the rich prosper. This is *not* what most thinking people want.

If you seriously want to find out what your friends and neighbours want, what do you do? You invite them for a chat over a drink or a meal . . . and then repeat the invitation as the conversation strengthens. Jesus said, 'For I was hungry and you gave me something to eat' (Matt. 25:35). Many people know they want something and are hungry with questions. The challenge is simple: feed them, listen to their questions and then, *when* they are ready, offer to feed them some answers, too.

8

Developing the Necessary Leadership

Whether it is in industry, education or the Christian church, the nature and style of the local, co-ordinating leadership is crucial to the organization's development and growth. Perhaps the key principle to hold in mind during this chapter is 'co-ordinating'.

In my eight years as a denominational training officer, I knew that my attitude and approach would colour the experience of everyone involved. Whether running retreats, evening courses, church weekends or pilgrimage tours, I always tried to work as part of a small but highly and similarly committed planning team. We then shared the public leadership of whatever the event or course we planned as well as in the encouragement of every participant's involvement.

It was important that that leadership shared itself around, whether at the communal meal tables or for whatever-the-conversation or country walks in our free time. Some years ago, I attended a highly publicized, major-input, well-attended Christian conference at the Swanwick Centre and, along with many others, I felt discomfited when publicly told a particular meal table was reserved for 'the elite leadership team', by the organizer's MC. How does that 'square' with the Jesus whom we read about in the New Testament? This was the same Jesus who made sure that he ate with tax-gatherers and sinners while also advising his followers about places at tables (Matt. 9:10; Luke 14:1–14).

My final two main chapters focus on the Christian grouping which is larger than the 'pocket' – or cell – group, or so-called table churches. Most of these latter have chosen fairly to limit their size to that of a front room or a dining table, before 'spawning off' another independent such gathering, like a strawberry runner. Those that federate together in some form, as Robert Banks's thesis[1] advocates, should find constructive suggestion about cross-cell forms of leadership. These chapters are about congregations, their vision and leadership.

So this chapter responds to some issues of the preceding chapter. It presupposes that if we are going to meet others' expectation of 'church', developing a Jesus community through sharing Christian hospitality, we have to know what we are aiming to build towards, create and potentially achieve. This is not meant to be a training manual for leadership. It is meant to offer some principles which local leadership teams need to contextualize for their own situations – and their own mutual learning.

Reviewing Patterns of Leadership

Christendom has much to answer for. Rightly, its defenders will claim that you cannot lay everything that is wrong with contemporary Christianity at Christendom's door. However, it was during the Christendom era that two decisive things occurred.

1. There was a shift to hierarchical models of church and ministry – whether conciliar or personal, creating the exercise of 'top down' authority.
2 There was an increasing acceptance of the Bible as a 'flat' document. Equal weight was afforded to both Testaments.

These two facts had profound implications for local congregations, their ministries and individual discipleship.

For radical Christians, the Bible cannot be a 'flat' document. For example, how can we say that the sometimes violent attitudes of the God in the *Hebrew* Testament can be given the same import as the Jesus who is Prince of Peace? How do we equate the decisive graciousness of Jesus' 'Go away and sin no more' with the retributive attitudes of Pentateuchal Law[2] towards the wrongdoer or those who were born as women or homosexual? If we believe in the grace of God, as revealed in Jesus, our discipleship will know that progression from violence to peace-making, from judgement to compassion and so on. Even if inherited or denominational movements still treat the Bible as 'flat', the advancing post-Christendom era demands a differential approach.

'Biblical morality is not found in the Ten Commandments but in the action of the Holy One.'[3] For radical Christians, the nature of that 'Holy One' can be supremely revealed only in the person and grace of Jesus. Christians are called to follow after Jesus in both personal daily discipleship and in the nature of the communities which gather to put his teaching into practice. Therefore, it must be Jesus' own pattern of leadership which we adopt if we are to heed the life-changing demand to live out his kingdom.

Models of leadership

Clearly the models of leadership in secular society – whether politics or business, be it Margaret Thatcher, Tony Blair, John Harvey-Jones or Alan Sugar – all present autocratic, individualistic personalities which some describe as strong leadership. Therefore it is hardly surprising to see such styles as the predominating pattern of the Christendom church, whether in prelates of the past or clergy of more recent times. Even the founders of radical Christian movements were strong individuals.

Although art may often portray St Francis as winsomely cradling doves, he must have had a tough constitution and personal discipline to advocate his patterns of simplicity of living. Early Anabaptist leaders appeared unafraid, in the face of their persecutors, torturers and executioners, in order to encourage other adherents to such discipleship. Perhaps the profession of lifelong vows by Taizé Brothers meant that Brother Roger, their prior, could exercise his leadership with an observed gentleness, although his personal counsel to many or his prophetic advocacy was unflinching in its biblical candour.

For any of us who personally met George MacLeod, the founder of the modern Iona Community, the experience was unforgettable. Whether it was after a thundering Sunday sermon or more quietly over a malt in his downstairs bedsit, George was never less than direct and incisive. Having known the privilege of working (over two decades) with John Vincent, the Ashram Community leader, makes me aware that those who work among the marginalized have to be robust characters to make their own and those marginalized voices heard within the inherited or historic denominational churches.

Inner strength and personal charisma, rather than idiosyncrasy, may have to be a mark of those who found, then lead alternative or radical gatherings of Christians. As these gatherings gain wider recognition as Jesus-shaped communities, they can become more easily prophetic for the whole inherited and not just the emerging church.

One role of this book must be to question whether an autocratic style is the only way. Even the most radical Christian leaders continually reflect on their conformity (often recognizing their lack of it) to Jesus' own pattern. Regrettably, I find less self-questioning in some of the leaders of the last generation's New Church movement and some of today's 'emerging church' leaders. All needed to have been personally and spiritually strong to step 'outside the box', but creating new wineskins is not an excuse for bossing the harvesters. How much do we fall short of the grace of God?

Models of ministry

John Howard Yoder, the most influential of the twentieth-century Mennonite theologians, wrote the following as a commentary on Ephesians 4. 'The Paul of Ephesians uses the term *the fullness of Christ* to describe a new mode of group relationships, in which every member of a body has a distinctly identifiable, divinely validated and empowered role.'[4] Brevity forbids a full hermeneutical analysis of this key New Testament passage in Ephesians 4. Verse 1 sets the gold standard: 'I urge you, imprisoned because I serve the Lord. Live your life so it measures up to that mark which God set in his calling to you' (author's translation). Then verses 3 and 5 command us to 'retain the harmony of the body', recognizing the role of the unifying Spirit, as we all serve one Lord, in proclaiming a single faith shared because of our common baptism – and I would want to add 'as believers' to the latter.

Personally, I believe the key section of Ephesians 4 is held within verses 11 to 13. This is an egalitarian vision of gifts and ministries. When working in congregational consultancy, I often paraphrase this teaching as the 'senders and the sent, the teachers and tea-makers, the pastors and the pray-ers'. Paul insists all these are needed to come equally together to 'build up the body of Christ' so that all may grow to a maturity of faith. This is a great vision of the community of Jesus – working, worshipping and witnessing in whatever context. It is also a timeless encouragement as we increasingly encounter post-Christendom attitudes in society and individuals.

In our post-Christendom context, it is right to note that Ephesians 4 is not the only model of extant ministry – even in Paul's own writing. A simple comparison of Philippians 1 and Ephesians 4 demonstrates these different patterns – the former greets the 'bishops' and their workers in Philippi whereas Ephesians refers to a less hierarchical model involving 'pastors' and 'deacons' or 'servers'. Banks helpfully delineates this further. He sees this as two different patterns of 'church ordering' which need continual re-application in the face of advancing post-Christendom.[5]

What is worth considering is the fact that the more radical and other Christians move *away* from a 'flat' interpretation of the Bible (i.e. treating all parts with equal worth), the more likely they are to move *towards* a 'flat', therefore less hierarchical and more egalitarian, view of ministry.

Strategic Vision-Making

How do you eat an elephant? One mouthful at a time. Very few people have the capacity to go from the A to Z of strategic vision-making in one move. Wise leadership will create the appropriate bite-size chunks for each developing step. Stuart Murray rightly suggests: 'Introducing café-style events or incorporating elements of alt.worship, [*sic*] for instance, will not produce post-Christendom churches. But this may stimulate journeys of discovery that will enable inherited churches to reflect more deeply on issues of culture and identify areas for further ecclesial and missional development.'[6] Murray's thesis sensibly demands that vision-making is accompanied by practical steps. Recall Emmanuel URC's Scones of Praise events (see Chapter 6) which built on enough folk memories and extant practical skills to build a new mission endeavour.

Strategic vision-making needs to be practical and involve as many folk as possible.

Working together

Wise leadership facilitates a programme of events, ranging from home groups through mission endeavours to need-oriented worship. Such leadership envisions this as part of a trajectory towards prayerfully discerned, co-ordinated congregational objectives. More will be said of such practical opportunities in the next chapter.

What is vital is that each 'activity' is planned by a group of folk, hopefully always including some of the wallflower-types who are often overlooked. As more things are prayerfully planned, and need to be planned, more people can be drawn into the planning and delivery of one-off events, recognizing these as pieces of an ongoing programme.

That collective approach must begin with a leadership. In church consultancy, I often heard ministers whinge about the fact that their PCC, deacons, stewards or elders either:

- Want to lord it over the individual minister,
  or
- Want to be treated simply as a sounding-board with few hands-on expectations.

Both of those moulds need to be broken on biblical grounds. 'The eldership, in the early church as in the synagogue, seems to have been plural, shared with a team of colleagues . . . Thus the ultimate impact of Paul's use of the body image is clearly and consistently antihierarchical.'[7]

It was the nature of the Christendom church to put clergy and ministers well up a hierarchical tree from which they must now climb down. Commissioned or ordained ministers *should not* play the game of 'being the martyr' but, in stepping aside, encourage their 'lay' colleagues in their leadership and gifts. We may not want a flat Bible but we must have an egalitarian leadership, in which everyone's gifts are equally respected, if we are to collectively develop both strategic and coherent vision.

Prayer and praxis

Strategic and coherent vision relies on two things: prayer and 'listening'. Each congregation needs to root its life and ministry in patterns of prayer: daily, personal and corporate. Anyone who has visited either East Asian 'cell church' conferences or the Canadian week-long church leaders' 'signs and wonders' seminars will know both can involve daily attendance at dawn prayer meetings. The explosive global growth of both movements tells of prayer's importance in vision and action. None of those patterns occurs without co-ordination.

For those with a more liberal Christian approach, the understanding of praxis, meaning a helix of action and reflection to enable progress along any trajectory, may be an easier touchstone. Each piece of action begins with reflective decision-making and afterwards turns to reflective review in order to improve the next piece of action. Prayer or spiritual reflection and action are two sides of the same coin for Jesus' disciples.

We must learn to listen:

1 For the voice of Jesus: Is what we believe we are being called towards consistent with the Jesus whom we discover and daily rediscover in the gospels?
2 What do our fellow-believers see as the positives and the pitfalls of what is being proposed?
3 We should ask: How is this 'event' going to reveal something more of the kingdom of God upon earth?
4 What in our local neighbourhood/town/city tells us that the proposed initiative has an automatic interface with what people are looking for?

Finally, two more selfish questions:

5 How will this 'event' enable more to receive the invitation of Jesus (that is, hospitality to a new life)? and
6 How will it make us more of a Jesus-shaped community?

Within post-Christendom, our vision will need to be more explicit, involving events or activities that are meeting known needs. This can be done most easily via hospitality, welcoming people into a non-threatening and non-judgemental community, where an easy interface can be created. 'Nurturing hospitality often involves nurturing a community life that sustains practitioners and creates a place into which outsiders want to come.'[8] For all that to work seamlessly, co-ordination is required.

Learning from others

Within historic monasticism, people travelled to monasteries, abbeys and minsters, whether for sanctuary or support, be that alms, medical help or spiritual need. Christian households, whether 'pockets' or part of a congregational network, need to review how they can exercise that hospitality and welcome. This can become the gateway into the kind of community of which most people have little or no experience.

'The monastic life remains as a testimony to the commitment to share, even though its forms cannot be a model for our society'; so runs the back cover of a new book,[9] which draws on the lessons of historic patterns of monasticism. Whether it is in 'new monasticism' conferences or the plethora of books appearing (such as the one quoted), there are good lessons to learn about the nature of hospitality and community for all Christians. What good leadership and advocacy must do is to learn how to adapt the richness and lessons of others' Christian discipleship, contextualizing it for each local situation in post-Christendom.

We must also learn to experience patterns of community afresh. An Anglican archdeacon friend spent over half of his recent sabbatical working residentially as a voluntary cleaner-kitchen hand in a Wiltshire retreat house. Several of my friends' children, with eco-sustainability concerns, have spent their gap years working as volunteers in local social projects or UK therapeutic communities. Friends in the Iona and Othona communities speak of the joy of many of their residential guests in sharing together in the household chores as an important part of community life. Vision-making is enhanced by experience.

But communities are not zoos where we go along to observe the inhabitants' interaction. Durnbaugh threads his way through the radical story of the Moravians from their eastern European beginnings.[10] True to their pattern elsewhere, Moravians developed 'settlements' – groups of small, simple family homes, clustered around vegetable gardens and a chapel – sometimes with a primary school too. During my adult life, I have been privileged to have Moravian acquaintances in their settlements at Droylsden, Manchester, and Pudsey, west Yorkshire. This model has much to commend it. But like the USA's Amish and Mennonite communities who live as 'the quiet in the land', so Moravians do in Britain and the rest of north-western Europe. It is beholden upon those of us in other radical traditions to encourage them to share the riches of their 'community vision' as a model for both us and the inherited church tradition. But Moravian settlements begin with a group of Christian disciples highly committed to their particular pattern of community. There cannot be a manual or international church conference to help others replicate that experience.

One size fits very few

Vision is bespoke – hardly ever off-the-peg. Despite the success of methodologies developed in Toronto or Singapore, they will have their 'ceilings' and limitations. One of Christendom's realities is that it tried to make Christianity become 'one size fits all'. Even after the Reformation with separate Protestant and (Roman) Catholic versions – both were still happy in their complicity with regional states.

Radical Christianity shared an alternative vision to that complicity. Radical faith was both bespoke and Jesus-shaped. The same bespoke and Jesus-shaped vision helps define the emerging church within Europe as the twenty-first century gets older.

In a post-modern, post-Christendom era, people will naturally question the grand overarching story or meta-narrative of the inherited church. Those whose strategic vision-making is not defined by some denominational authority of the past centuries may well gain a better hearing. Which would you prefer: an invitation to go to church on a busy Sunday or a supper invitation on a mutually convenient date?

Co-ordinated and strategic vision-making now will let go of much past practice and reach out to people in ways that are comfortable and hospitable. This will help create a new Jesus-styled community. Walter Brueggemann often says, 'We are called to abandon and embrace.'[11] In other words, do not be held by

Christendom styles, and accept new ways of becoming Jesus-shaped communities.

Developing Post-Christendom Leadership

Each writer in this *After Christendom* series is committed to nurturing and encouraging authentic discipleship. Also each *After Christendom* writer has been profoundly influenced by the Anabaptist witness, both historically and contemporarily.

Having been raised in that Anabaptist stream of life and witness, then as an adult having found its leadership patterns to be the most conducive to developing creativity and missional congregations, I cannot but write from this experience. Within the Anabaptist movement, we recognize that 'the vitality of the church depends upon leadership' is a key principle.

The After Christendom *experience*

In one of the seminal *After Christendom* volumes, Stuart Murray wrote a short section about leadership.[13] One predictable response and another more widespread response occurred. Predictably, each of the succeeding volumes has needed to address the 'leadership question' from that volume's perspective.

But for Murray, myself and others in the Anabaptist tradition, his *Church after Christendom* ignited a series of requests to facilitate teaching and the understanding of the gifts of this radical stream. This became the widespread response even if the growing number of requests continues as a joyful surprise. For me, this has meant teaching local church leaderships (often residentially), leading clergy seminars and day conferences as well as conducting interactive preaching series and/or sharing in consultancy with local congregations.

Therefore, I shall take up four of Murray's key leadership points, commenting upon them before offering some further reflections of my own.

The role of leaders

In the gospels we see Jesus exercising collaborative ministry in sending out the disciples (Luke 9:1-6; 10:1–12). Was it just economy of personnel which meant they worked in pairs? The discussion above of Ephesians 4 is highlighted for contemporary ministry by Murray: 'The role of leaders in post-Christendom churches – operating accountably in a team context with others whose gifts and perspectives are different – is to empower rather than perform, develop processes to sustain the community and equip those who are really on the front line.'[14] 'Front line' needs to be understood as those Christians working in non-church environments, where they are seen as individuals-with-skills first, then perhaps as Christians if their lives, prayer and attitudes so 'shine through'.

Although I knew this, I had not quite realized how stark this is, until I retired away from my role as 'the minister of . . . ' Now, whether in school governance or NHS appeal circles, people prefer to introduce or address me as 'Dr Francis' rather than 'Revd Francis' (even if my personal preference is for Andrew Francis). This may tell us something more of that post-Christendom shift, that their world-view considers doctors and academics are either more socially acceptable or preferable to clergy.

Facilitators or leaders

Clearly the whole, and not just the radical, church needs to respect gifts and ministries more than titles or seminary-trained professional church-people, if it is to develop holistic mission and grass-roots Jesus-shaped communities. 'In post-Christendom, we must *reconfigure* and *de-emphasize* leadership if churches are to be harmonious and healthy.'[15]

We can learn from the experience of the lay-led 'cell church movement', which is fast-growing in the sophisticated highly urbanized cities of east Asia, such as Singapore. There, patterns of mentoring mean that each cell is led by a locally trained couple, assisted by two others, who are all mentored weekly in addition to their cell meeting. A criticism may be made of its pyramid structure, but it works. Emmanuel's recreated home-group strategy, explained in Chapter 4, was modelled on this pattern – and here in suburban Britain, it worked. We need to move away from patterns of hierarchical or supervisory leadership towards nurturing group facilitators. 'Where pastors encourage the congregation as a whole to get together in more interactive ways, they will begin to experience some redefinition of their role.'[16]

What are 'we' training people to do?
Those who select and train leaders face the challenge of prioritiz-
ing the skills needed for future church over those that have
served inherited churches well. Networkers, community theologians, team-builders, spiritual directors, mentors, coaches and
trainers who equip others may be more valuable than public per-
formers.'[17] While these titles cannot occur except in the most
liberally paraphrased version of Ephesians 4, the point is made.
Not a single mention of 'bishops, priests and deacons' or regional ministers, even evangelists. Should Methodism still require
every prospective minister to be a fully qualified local preacher?
Should every Anglican ordinand be normally expected to 'serve
their title' in a well-ordered parish context?

A past lesson from the New Churches, and now from the
'emerging churches' is that in these groups' naissance, they are
not usually led by 'church professionals' but by Christians earning their living in secular employment. Elsewhere, I have advocated that as we move into post-Christendom all church leaders
should be *at least* bi-vocational – earning at least part of their
living in a secular context.[18]

Training for all!
At the start of this chapter, I wrote of my work as a training officer. Leading clergy conferences and reading parties is enjoyable
and intellectually stimulating. The bigger challenge lies in the
provision of opportunities for those earning their living in secular employment, the retired and the home-based (whether par-
enting or unemployed). 'If post-Christendom churches are to
become multi-gifted communities, and the mature church
[which] Ephesians 4 envisages is to evolve or emerge, training for
all (not just leaders) is essential.'[19]

Although I already knew this, we had to demonstrate it. We
responded practically, showing by experience and example, that
'one size fits all' programmes will not meet the rapidly changing
local contexts of post-Christendom. In developing courses in
which we learned new things *together* or shared worship and mission experiences, excitement, commitment and numbers grew. As
we nurtured lay congregational leadership, more traditional
churches seeing the growth which these lay-ministries brought,

challenged the denomination regionally to amend its recognized patterns of leadership.

However what was, and still is, the most formative for all (including me) is when a series of whole-congregation (or multi-cell) events work, to meet not just their needs but the vision which they discern God is calling them towards. This kind of co-ordinated approach works.

Learning from our experiences

'The challenge to the early Christians was to redeem a network of existing relationships; our challenge is generally to create community where little has existed before.'[20] We are not called to inappropriate replication of the New Testament congregations but to explore a 'new wineskins' vision that has sufficient joined-up thinking and biblical basis to speak and gather others within the post-Christendom context.

As some full-time clergy and ministers read that last sentence, they will howl that this is what they are continually doing, day after day, week after week. Some may have to recognize that their efforts are just not appreciated. Pause.

- Think of Jesus' ministry with the disciples; it was itinerant, coming into a neighbourhood community offering preaching, teaching and healing while receiving local hospitality.
- Read Acts again. Recognize that Luke identifies both the 'settled' ministries of the Jerusalem church's leaders as well as Paul's and others' itinerancy, which served the local, lay-led, newly planted emerging churches.
- Reading the rest of the New Testament, you can see similar trends in the Pastoral Epistles and the Letters of John.

The New Testament teaches that the input given by itinerant leaders to local and emerging churches, capably lay-led, provided the stimulus for growth and mission. But this would have relied on the hospitality to such leaders from that congregation, who would have needed to gather as and be community (not just a Sunday congregation) to share together in that intensive teaching and prayer over a few days or possibly weeks. This seems in sharp contrast to the inherited Christendom model of congregations being led by a (often) solo, paid, college-trained professional. But these latter ministers also rely on the institutional hospitality of their congregations to pay their diocesan or denominational quotas.

The lessons of radical church history (recall Chapter 2) echo New Testament patterns. To utilize the traditions which I know best:

- Menno Simons and other Anabaptist pioneers continually moved around the northern Netherlands, both evading their persecutors but more importantly encouraging the developing Anabaptist pockets, cells and congregations (ultimately these became the start of the Mennonite movement).
- My own great-grandfather was a travelling evangelist in the Anabaptist-style Restorationist movement (becoming known as the Churches of Christ rather than as Campbellites), who planted churches after running tent missions, returning months later, then for shorter periods in successive years, to nurture and train their local leaders.
- My own experience in a lifetime of denominational (United Reformed Church) ministry was facilitated by its monthly stipend – even if for nearly two-thirds of that service, I was seconded part-time elsewhere as a broadcaster, lay-trainer, church consultant and so on.
- Menno Simons, my great-grandfather and many others relied on the hospitality of often very poor folk to enable their ministries to bear fruit, new lay leadership to be encouraged and congregations to be planted, then grow. It also needed the sense of community from daily dawn prayer meetings, and house groups meeting every few days, to enable such itinerant leaders' ministries to be effective.

Those inherited congregations which survive into post-Christendom may well find their teams' leaders are predominantly self-supporting, drawing on itinerant facilitators to encourage new opportunities for work and witness.

Learning afresh

What the various Pilgrim groups demonstrated is that lay leaders need a secure place to feel welcome, receive hospitality, experience some community and confidentially share their struggles prayerfully. In each, I never sought to be the leader but merely the host whenever Pilgrim met in my home.

Honing my cooking skills over a lifetime has never been a chore, given the number of appreciative guests in my home. But I have also acquired other skills. I undertook obtaining statutorily required food hygiene certificates in order to lead the catering teams for congregational and other public events.

I am still improving my IT skills so that I can pitch up with USB pens to training events and not appear as the Luddite I would prefer to be. I have adopted a consistent pattern of highlighting every book I read, in order to draw on its resource and teaching more quickly. In the days before Tippex, I had grown up making final text-notes on a typewriter and writing only erasable pencil notes in book margins. I am learning afresh.

Becoming a learner in a variety of contexts becomes helpful when one is invited to understand others as one is invited to facilitate their learning, growth and discipleship.[21]

Learning is part of lifelong discipleship. Pastors and ministers are called to both accept and model that, rejecting the notion that learning finishes with the return of the last book to the seminary library. That is not a joke. Sadly, I remember one best-unnamed seminary lecturer announcing that 'We will give you every tool which you will need for lifelong ministry'. How regrettable and how Christendom is that? It assumed that neither church nor ministry would change in our working lives.

Peter was always the big fisherman. Simon the Zealot was a political agitator. Levi, the tax-gatherer, would always be deemed a collaborator. We can only be what we are – until the Spirit of Jesus turns us around. The Greek words for 'conversion' is *metanoia*; it literally means 'to turn around'. It is the grace of God which transforms our personal sinfulness.

Ministry in post-Christendom should not be conducted from pedestals – it is easy to fall off. I have just persuaded a Methodist minister friend to *not* title his retirement memoir *The Ebullient Churchman* – that speaks of a Christendom priority which was certainly not the mark of his gracious ministry. We have to be Jesus' disciples each and every day, and no clerical collar nor episcopal purple can change that demand.

From the heart of the modern Anabaptist movement, Jeffrey Schrag, the General Secretary of the USA's General Conference Mennonite Church (the then biggest Anabaptist global grouping), said in 1997 of their leaders: 'It is *who you are*, much more than what you do in ministry, that will count.'[22] That became a key Mennonite principle of congregational mentoring.

As with vision-making, ministry in post-Christendom will be increasingly bespoke, recognizing far more gifts and ministries than inherited churches used to. Such ministry will be far more coherent with New Testament practice, becoming contextualized and Spirit-led. If we are to emerge from the wilderness of post-Christendom, Christians will need to root their lives in prayer, live more simply and confront the wild beasts of Christendom attitudes. The best place to do that will be together, whether in congregations or 'pockets' committed to sharing more of life's journey.

Can We Teach Old Dogs?

I was one of those trained to preach in that doctrinaire, alliterative, three-point-sermon way mentioned in Chapter 7. I had to listen to better preachers, and learn from them and my own reading about how to deliver both narrative sermons and homilies – necessary for those 9:00 a.m. Communions, followed by breakfast.

I have been fortunate to have spent the whole of my adult life with some involvement in popular, normally local broadcasting. There, I had to learn to deliver accurately timed 'thoughts for the day' and three-sentence interview answers to tough moral questions, among several skills. But most of all it has been my parallel (to stipendiary ministry in an inherited denomination) journey, within any number of Anabaptist contexts and networks, which has challenged afresh. It caused me to recognize that my seminary-based training ill-equipped me for life in the post-Christendom landscape.

There will be those from my early denominational pastorates who *may* accuse me of playing the 'ministerial game'. But there will be many more who can witness to my efforts to encourage collaborative and multi-voiced leadership teams. When I left theological college in 1982, the valedictory service included a senior denominational figure preaching to us that we were to be 'the bottom-line leaders' for our churches, as though we were to become the CEOs of those patient congregations. I knew then that my calling was different. Although I might be stipendiary (i.e. paid), I wanted to be a teaching resource and a worship facilitator even if, also, I had to be the pastoral coordinator, programme organizer and general factotum.

In working to move towards my sense of calling, as well as to reject the expected other model, I had to learn that such church leaders are Christendom-focused, having been trained by others whose theology and attitudes are rooted between the World Wars. Now thirty years on, I am learning to develop the ministry to which I was called back then.

This is not 'business as usual'

Taking time was a luxury that I used to have. The post-Christendom agenda is now upon us with far more urgency than it was thirty years ago. But every congregation needs to take the luxury of time, in their own way, to discern vision and listen *with* a multi-voiced team of leaders. 'Weekend retreats with plenty of time for rest and fun mixed with inspiration may be a way of rekindling their interest and commitment'[23] for the bruised and disillusioned with failing inherited or denominational patterns. Although not all congregations can afford mountain or rural retreats or weekends away, the Emmanuel model described earlier offers such an alternative. When I worked in industrial mediation, my mentor taught me that 'quality time means quality decisions'. Good leaders never rush the process of vision-making. Jesus spent years with his disciples helping them understand something of the kingdom.

A congregation's 'ethos is also critical for nurturing counter-cultural discipleship and creating missional communities to incarnate the gospel creatively and winsomely in the strange new world of post-Christendom'.[24] It is how we make this pertinent observation come alive which will determine the shape of a congregation's mission. Then it can exercise a true and gracious welcome in its hospitality, enabling another Sunday congregation authentically to become a 24/7 further outpost community of the kingdom.

It is a facilitational challenge to any form of plural or solo leadership to help that group of Christians re-envision its life to be more truly Jesus-shaped. As Walter Brueggemann reminds us, within post-Christendom 'our faith comes to fullness as we are teased to think new thoughts, as our imagination is lured beyond "business as usual"'.[25]

9

Developing the 'Building-Blocks'

'It does seem in our countries in Britain, especially in England and Wales, that Christianity, as a sort of backdrop to people's lives and moral decisions – and to the Government, to the social life of the country – has now almost vanished.'[1] These words from Cardinal Cormac Murphy O'Connor, then Cardinal Archbishop of Westminster, heralded his keynote address to the National Conference of Catholic Priests in Leeds in September 2001.

This description declares advancing post-Christendom. It is also telling because it came from a leader of one of the global participants in Christendom. Even for them, advancing post-Christendom cannot be ignored. Strategically, each Catholic diocese has been reviewing its mission needs, reducing buildings to key core locations of Catholic population.

In the intervening decade Catholic bishops, spokesmen and local clergy have increasingly spoken of Britain becoming a mission field afresh. That statement, as Anabaptist-influenced writers of this *After Christendom* series recognize, invites wide recognition of the mission challenge which post-Christendom has stealthily brought to north-western Europe.

In reading the previous chapter, how often did 'co-ordination' come to mind? Unless vision and action are co-ordinated in some helical praxis, no organization will make forward progress.

Unless a leadership, solo or team, co-ordinate the efforts of the workforce, 'their labours will be in vain'. A near-neighbour with Parkinson's disease knows that without his daily medication, his bodily co-ordination falters horribly. Every Christian community knows that without co-ordination its life together falters, and probably stalls (if not destroys) its mission purpose. Whether that is at the local independent congregational level or that of a global denominational policy such as the Roman Catholic Church now perceives it needs, co-ordination is required.

This chapter considers some of the building-blocks necessary to facilitate the growth of a Christian community from a Sunday congregation. It would be a very brave inherited or denominational church leader who split up their congregation into quasi-independent pocket-sized emerging churches. Although I am aware of two such New Churches in northern England which did this, nearly twenty years ago, to great missionary effect, perhaps the fact that all their leadership team earned their income outside the congregations made it an easier decision.

Recognizing the Need for Change

Congregations are planted and some congregations die, fail or are closed. This is a fact of faith, which may be due to issues of social or urban engineering and/or changing demography as well as any spiritual malaise. So some churches will die because new road networks or housing projects obliterate the building which they work from. Some will also die because they are not prepared to try anything new. Sadly the old joke about the last seven words of the church, as the final trumpet sounds, 'We've never done it like this before' are true. Some will die through lack of mission which means the congregation simply ages into the 'ten green bottles syndrome' until their viability is lost through lack of numbers. There is hope.

'We've never done it like this before'

While a few may suggest that every congregation must repent of their Christendom past and change, such a call is foolish. Both emerging churches and inherited or denominational leaders and councils need to stand with so-called traditional congregations and encourage them to make a transition appropriate to their context.

Against the grey background of a wintry Danish coast, the film *Babette's Feast* speaks of how a French housekeeper spends all her lottery winnings on a sumptuous feast. This meal is served to her austere employers, two spinster sisters, and their guests. The sisters are the daughters of the late founding-pastor of a now dying sect. Apart from one outside guest, no one really appreciates the sacrifice and challenge involved to turn their world back into a technicolour experience from its monochrome ways. *Babette's Feast* is a parable for the church – unless we find the way to enthuse the outsiders towards commitment, the church becomes greyer, colder and begins to die.

The needs will be as different between urban, multi-ethnic, multicultural settings and rural Middle England as between some countries. This will require:

- More bespoke responses,
- More encouragement of creative vision-making,
- Better development of team leadership,
- The willingness to take risks as well as fund new initiatives,
- Contextual co-ordination.

Both the Anglican and subsequently the Methodist Churches are to be encouraged in their development of the Fresh Expressions initiative, to enable inherited congregations to explore patterns of transition, facilitating local 'fresh expressions' of church. The United Reformed Church in 2009 was the first national denomination to appoint an 'Emerging Church Advocate', allowing her to be based in a small Devon town both to develop an 'emerging church' there but also to travel, to teach and encourage others to create quasi-independent groups.

Perhaps the past opprobrium towards the pioneering work of Ivor Smith Cameron in London[2] or David Cave in Liverpool[3] should be remembered, even repented of, as inherited Christendom movements look askance at some of the newer, emerging models. Using the lessons and examples of recent denominational history are ways in which traditionally oriented local church councils, such as PCCs, elders or deacons, or stewards' meetings, can be enabled to reflect upon their own prejudice towards change.

But first, you have to get them to talk about their concerns and worries. When I worked with one very stilted congregation as its

minister, I invited each of the leaders with their partners or
spouses for a meal. I began with the church secretary and church
treasurer. During the course of each subsequent evening, I asked
those who came to share not only their hopes and dreams but
also their fears for the congregation. After my guests left and
before the washing-up, I made copious notes of their comments.
Both the fear of failure and a lifelong privatized faith were
expressed as strongly as any fear of change or new things. Since
that experience, I have worked similarly with over twenty
congregations, over meals, gaining almost the same findings vir-
tually every time. Perhaps, note how this strategic use of hospitality built relationships and enabled both future prayers and
co-ordinated planning.

Following my advice, an Anglican priest-friend adopted this
pattern too. He invited his two churchwardens first, then his PCC
members in turn and discovered similar emotions, findings and
trends. His experience led both him and me to encourage other
Anglican incumbents to adopt this model. Partly due to this 'success', my friend has now become a part-time diocesan training
officer. Pastors and preachers need to begin helping folk to be not
just believers but disciples, encouraging sufficient confidence to
follow Jesus. But first we must listen to them and understand
their fears.

Letting go of our past – graciously!

Part of this past fear of failure has been the Christendom acceptance of 'churchianity' or Sunday Christianity. This is just going to
church whether weekly, monthly or annually, plus occasionally
saying prayers behind closed doors at home. This does not measure up to what discipleship is, as this book has emphasized.

Post-Christendom will demand a vibrancy and confidence in
the life and conversation of those who choose to follow Jesus. In
the Great Commission, Jesus said, 'Go to everyone, wherever
they are, then make them my disciples, baptizing them in my
name and teaching them to do everything which I have told you'
(Matt. 28:19–20, author's translation). I often begin local church
leaders' away-days by inviting them to discuss three ways in
which their congregation lives that commission and three ways
in which they do not. As an icebreaker, it gets them creatively

started as well as recognizing three things: their hopes, their fears and Jesus' benchmark challenge.

In the face of post-Christendom, Christians must learn to perceive, then determine their agenda prayerfully, building both vision and strategy upon that. An Anglican friend of mine who recently moved from an inner-city parish to a rural East Anglian town, expressed surprise when he was asked to chair a town-wide public meeting, just because he was the town's vicar. His surprise, as a vicar, at such a rare occurrence demonstrates urban society's increasing shift away from Christendom.

No longer can any church just assume that others will be interested automatically in the church's agenda or the vital call to become disciples of Jesus. Once we (radical, emerging and inherited Christians) and as many other churchgoers recognize that, hope can be restored. Then new mission opportunities can be created in any and every kind of neighbourhood. So we can find the courage to let go of our past and previously failing ways of 'doing church'.

Hospitality

Recently, a West Midlands congregation decided to revamp their buildings for neighbourhood use. Using an external consultant, they conducted both a parish and a mission audit. Bravely, they condensed these findings into a self-produced colour brochure with decent-size print, community perceptions and good photographs. Impressively, they then not only mobilized their congregation to host either tea parties or wine-and-cheese evenings in a wide spread of local homes but also encouraged them to give invitations to their friends and neighbours in their own street. At each such party, the brochures were given out, one of the leaders spoke and invited every participant to ask questions and make responses to help the church reshape their buildings. Already, before definitive building plans have been submitted, neighbourhood folks are coming again to Sunday worship and the congregation has grown by about 10 per cent. Hospitality communicates.

Nearly all emerging churches use food and/or summer barbecues as focuses for gathering. A nearby house was tenanted, and the new tenants came round to invite us to their house-warming barbecue 'Just so we can get to know folks'. They are not Christians but their invitation was natural and everyday in its approach. Churches need to look at not attempting to do too much as they seek to build relationships, to let them grow at their own pace, in their own time. A fellow speaker at a recent evangelists' conference wisely said, 'Don't drive a ten-ton piece of witness over a one-ton relationship.' How right he is – and how often has the church lost out to inappropriate patterns of personal evangelism?

The examples in the above few paragraphs tell us that both natural returnees to Sunday worship and the need for good evangelistic practice are timely reminders of what local congregations need to rediscover.

Even if by this point you are still questioning how much post-Christendom is either advancing or is a serious threat to the UK church's status quo, my ongoing contention is that post-Christendom has arrived. Its influence will grow, with the danger of overwhelming an unsuspecting church. Therefore, we need to find ways of building on the strengths of inherited or denominational churches to enable the necessary transmutation for the next generations.

While that happens, Christian leaders need willingly, with prayerful support, to let people go who have gained or been given a vision for an alternative pattern of missionary gathering, whether or not we call it 'emerging church'.

Building on our strengths

Build on your strengths. This will mean both taking old and making new initiatives.

All denominational ministers will recognize the trade in women's meeting appointments. Often these midweek gatherings draw some who do not or cannot attend Sunday worship but have a deep sense of fellowship and community about them as real care is given: 'Does anyone know why Hilda isn't here today?' Normally, the participants have far closer, even if only via weekly meeting, bonds with one another, than happens in the regular Sunday morning congregation. Delving further, one discovers that many of these groups began as young wives' groups, trading chat, recipes and baby clothes, maturing via 'the Thursday group', into the women's meeting as widowhood, old age and isolation beckon. Their talks-and-outings agenda, always accompanied by tea and biscuits, and very often by regular prayer for one another, can form great outreach opportunities. In several congregations women's meetings have been the start of renewed interest and attendances. Regrettably, there is little parallel in men's gatherings.

Whether it is in the women's meeting, midweek children's activity or another specific part of the local congregation's programme, there are opportunities to build links back to folk locally. This is particularly true where there is 'low threshold'; for example, no large doctrinal questions. Identifying those opportunities may begin with a single conversation over a cup of tea with any of the programme's leaders. Hospitality works.

Build on your strengths – look at the neighbourhood community again.

- What groups of local residents are there and with what social needs?
- Do not be frightened of spending money – pay for a recommended person to help you undertake a mission audit.
- Learn afresh about your neighbourhood – stop just lamenting, 'It was better when . . .'
- Which local groups need public premises to further their work? Be hospitable and offer them space at subsidized rates.

Take heart from others' initiatives

I know of formerly struggling congregations in Birmingham, Coventry and Manchester, on the edge of the student quarters. Each has revitalized its life with a weekly free soup-and-bread lunch during term-times. All are attracting sufficient students on Sundays to start a lunch with an elder-led discussion group. One congregation had grateful students repaint their 'fellowship room' and carry in from around the corner the redundant chairs being discarded by a closing day centre.

One West Yorkshire congregation, with the support of the local imam, hosted a midweek women's gathering: 'in which the "white British" taught English and the Asian women taught

them their forms of cookery', they told me. Many of those attendees are now being drawn into more of that congregation's
activities.

Barbara Glasson has recounted the story of Liverpool's 'Bread
Church' in which the single, unemployed or isolated gather several times per week to bake bread – each person baking an extra
loaf to give away.[4]

Many day-trippers from Largs to the Isle of Cumbrae still
buy their lunch from the local bakery. This was started and
then run by the Community of Celebration while they had
their home there. When they moved on, the bakery was given
to the islanders. So now, a generation onwards, locals still tell
the story of how that Jesus community transformed island
life.

An East Midlands town church opened its basement each
weekday for homeless men. After a few months, they began to
find these same men queuing at the door for Sunday worship.
Some were further helped to find accommodation locally and
two have joined the church.

One London Mennonite, who had trained as a baker, moved
to Carmarthenshire and started a solar-powered bakery. It is
now well-known beyond that region and could sell twice as
much quality bread as it produces. Talking to the baker, he
speaks of a vibrant faith, with his Anabaptist 'bread for all' and
'treading lightly upon the land' theology of eco-justice. Like
Christians who run commercial cafés (referred to in Chapter 6),
the 'small is beautiful' principle can be a form of business
attracting others.

During December 2011, the BBC told of the church in Bedale
which reopened the village bakery, training folk to work in it.
Despite the church almost scuppering the project by 'moving on'
the visionary curate who led the work, the local responses to the
church have been transformed for the good.

All of these example, involve everyday food – often bread. For
several years, the poet Joy Mead spoke of the social and spiritual
significance of bread, encouraging her audiences to be hospitable
in their baking.[5] Simple hospitality can create good community.
Meals are a place where most people happily engage in conversation. Talk helps build relationships.

Rethink old practices

In post-Christendom, in their programmes, styles, worship and buildings churches will be far more differently bespoke than the 'there's the church, there's the steeple' one-size-fits-all children's rhyme reflecting Christendom's mentality.

When a preacher stands at the front of Sunday worship, she or he sees expectant faces – even if very few. People are a strength of the Jesus community. A good 'test' of any act of worship or preacher's words will be how animatedly the people leave afterwards. Is it relief at leaving, or because they have been encouraged and freshly envisioned?

In the Free Church tradition, there is something called the 'church meeting'. It is often a moribund business meeting. Together with a friend I devised a series of games to utilize in each church meeting, to be split by refreshments including a tasting of world food or Mrs Bloggs's latest and much-appreciated cake recipe. In each of our congregations, numbers grew at these important gatherings as people felt valued as they became again truly the church *meeting* – encountering another, with laughter, conversation and some tasty nibbles.

We have to find ways of enabling our Sunday congregations to become 'Jesus communities' afresh through an a-b-c progression rather than via an A to Z leap. It will mean creating increasing patterns of sharing. Both developing multi-voiced Sunday worship and enabling real people-oriented encounters in any growing midweek activity are needed.

When one multi-racial London 'emerging church' wanted to repeat a 'justice event', they partnered with an inherited church to mount a ticketed supper during Christian Aid Week. Those on the central table were served a three-course meal. Those around the edge were served a filling peasant meal with bread or rice, before a cogent speaker explained the world's inequalities and their Christian commitments in tackling world poverty. Both the 'emerging' and 'inherited' churches had new folk join them as a result. Despite the concept being a variation on an old theme, the partnership and the necessary hospitality spoke to newcomers about God's justice.

Practical discipleship rather than 'privatized faith' will be the mark of post-Christendom Jesus communities. That may begin with welcoming each other, sometimes defined as being hospitable.

Chianti and chips

The first Christian converts were reminded to 'practise hospitality' (Heb. 13:2).

There is hardly a British community where there is not some level of exercising hospitality between friends and neighbours. The key is to tap into this appropriately. It would be stupid to impose a dinner-party mentality upon a pie-and-chip-supper neighbourhood or vice versa.

One problem is that most Christendom church leaders (and their partners or spouses) have either come from or been expected to be at the dinner-party end of the social spectrum. What about being 'all things to all men' (1 Cor. 9:22), eating 'whatever is set before you' (Luke 10:8) or being accused of eating with tax-gatherers and sinners (Matt. 9:11)? Utilize the meals pattern of the local social style to foster friendships between church members.

In suburban situations, I have encouraged safari suppers, with drinks and nibbles in one household, starters in another, main course in the next and dessert and coffee at the last, while encouraging all those dining to offer the ingredients of dishes (by pre-arrangement) to the various hosts, as well as help and support. I am aware of an emerging church on the south coast which came together as first two, then three couples, hosted safari suppers.

On a London Tube journey yesterday, an advert proclaimed: 'The family that eats together, stays together' offering an eating therapy course from a secular counselling service. Eating together fosters a sense of family. Christians in their local communities need to foster a sense of family. Point made.

During summer months, I have encouraged congregations to hold a summer programme, using a common theme drawing together Sunday worship and a midweek social. The programme's aim was to encourage 'the bringing of friends'. One summer's theme was 'Mediterranean journeys' based on Paul's missionary travels. Its Roman week featured Italian pastimes, Chianti and chips. It was so popular and oversubscribed that we had to repeat it in the autumn. My then co-pastor now has three winter Chianti-and-chips evenings when someone speaks about their foreign travels to this growing group. For several, this group rather than Sunday worship has been the way into 'church'. Inherited churches have to find ways to get folks over the threshold and into conversation.

A growing number of congregations with fortnightly house groups encourage their members to use 'just one other' evening per month to host a supper party – once for folk from the congregation and the alternating monthly occasion for their own non-Christian, unchurched or dechurched contacts. As post-Christendom bites, and fewer of our contacts and neighbours may know anything about Jesus and his community, such hospitality builds bridges.

Eating together or entertaining

At a mission conference, I was asked to deliver a seminar about 'non-competitive hospitality' to explain that Christian discipleship does not mean trying to outclass the previous host. Why not discuss a standard at the church meeting and encourage everyone to generally follow that pattern? Despite their faults, Amish communities share the practice of non-competitive communal meals, with each family bringing food to the community's accepted level to share.

Also within the Anabaptist spectrum, North American Mennonites have creatively developed further patterns of shared or potluck meals as well as home-catering traditions. Many of their best-loved cookery writers shun the word 'entertaining' for those whom 'they invite over for supper', preferring to involve 'guests' in salad preparation, bread-cutting and conversation rather than holding them at arm's length.[6]

Check out your own food style. It is not just my Anabaptist heritage which makes me see the wisdom of so valuing our guests that we prefer to spend time with them in conversation rather than faffing over cordon bleu finishes to dinner-party standards. We far prefer to utilize casserole meals, oven-bakes or roasts; a steamer for vegetables to ease serving meals; accompanied by bread (home-made!), pasta or rice; and with an easy dessert. Easy winter lunches with colleagues – of a hearty home-made soup with bread, and fruit or yoghurt for dessert – enhance rather than interrupt the conversation.

Catering simply in a way that reflects the needs of the world is an act of Christian witness, too. In post-Christendom, the nature of our witness, our welcome and our catering style speaks of our faith and becomes even more important as testimony. Consider that local Christian Aid Week event a few paragraphs ago.

Use church away-days and occasional extra congregational meals to practise bring-and-share hospitality; use sign-up lists to avoid wasteful duplication but with enough options to allow some to afford what they bring without embarrassment (e.g. bread, crisps, fruit juices). Importantly, away-days are great learning times, teaching us how to be aware of others' needs in many ways, including for example disability or dietary restrictions. Away-days do need to be really 'away', so that folk are not tempted to 'just pop home', but it does not need to cost the earth.

One Leicester congregation partnered a nearby rural church, hosting each other's away-days on consecutive Saturdays. Previously the two leadership teams had met and agreed on similar levels of catering provision: both congregations used Richard Gillard's 'servant' hymn to symbolize their new relationship.[7] Away-days offer the ideal opportunity to plan a piece of mission strategy, enabling many to express their concerns as well as their hopes, and learning that providing good hospitality helps.

Thinking outside whose box?

Strategically, after a number of 'tried and tested' models – perhaps following an example from this book – have successfully worked as confidence-builders, it becomes time to 'think outside the box' – a hackneyed but helpful phrase. One of the best seminary epithets given to us all was: 'You have two ears and one mouth, use them in that proportion.' The same is true when introducing new ideas or mission activities – mix them up in good proportion with other confidence-builders. Remember that the aim of this section is to help inherited congregations transmute into a more coherent Jesus-shape to meet post-Christendom's challenges.

One west London congregation gathered a small team of proficient amateur cooks who opened a temporary Christmas restaurant on their church premises for four consecutive nights after Boxing Day. Knowing the cooks' high standards, other church members brought and paid for their friends to come and eat a restaurant-quality four-course dinner with coffee. Not only did various Third World charities benefit from the four-figure profit made each evening, but also nearly everyone who came for a meal has returned to that local church since, whether for a concert, midweek activity or Sunday worship. Redeeming the church's dry fusty image will also build bridges.

Taking his cue from the Netherbow, an Edinburgh theatre with a reputation for hosting quality questioning drama, one Scottish minister in a tourist area saw possibilities in his refurbished church buildings to host drama, using the central spotlit space (having moved the Communion table out of the way). Wise planning included: Holy Week gospel monologues, the use of good local amateur companies, and well-performed versions of Ewan Hooper's *A Man Dies*. These events and other plays drew crowds, gospel interest and joy from many locally. Sadly, there were those occasional churchgoers who caused enough criticism to end the experiment and the disillusioned minister moved on; hence anonymity here.

Creating such fine post-Christendom initiatives can have high costs, emphasizing the need for good vision-making, strategic preparation and the co-ordination of both congregation and vision. But it will also require congregations to think beyond their usual parameters. Once that is achieved, they have to gain enough confidence and courage to enable others to think beyond their 'traditional church' preconceptions. My latter two examples were high-profile; both worked but with different results.

Unless it is a 'pocket' of Christians inviting their known contacts, friends and neighbours home for supper, congregations working to attract attention in a multi-media age must recognize 'make do and mend' is simply not good enough for the majority of others to bother with us. *Either* we have to be truly alternative or radical, calling people to simplicity and downshifting, *or* we are going to be competing in a highly professionalized world, full of restrictive legislation.

My preference for most congregations has to be the former 'simplicity options' or possibly some middle ground such as

Emmanuel's Scones of Praise, which for some might be as daring as they can manage to be.

Community

In the last main chapter of a volume such as this, I must still define what I mean when 'community' is written about. Perhaps it is easier to say what it is not.

Discerning vocation or calling

Brevity precludes this volume from offering either serious comment or practical advice to those seeking to explore a lifetime vocation within a historic, professed (one with lifelong vows) religious community. There can be no substitute for such people corresponding with the guest-master or novice-mistress of such Orders and requesting to spend increasing times of retreat at their mother houses. For those with a notion of such vocation, the writings of either Christopher Jamison[8] or Brother Roger of Taizé[9] may provide some avenues to assist discernment.

There are those predominantly lay residential communities which come together around annually or periodically professed vows of mutual accountability and trust. Just like several of the historic monastic communities, they generate income for their 'common purse' by members working either within their own industries or for outside employers. Already in Chapter 3, we have referred to the successful example of the Jesus Fellowship based at Bugbrooke in Northamptonshire; they are often also known as the 'Jesus Army' because of their commonly worn multi-coloured coats, when conducting mission-on-the-streets activities. Another successful lay, residential version is the conference-centre community, exemplified by Lee Abbey in north Devon, but the necessarily hierarchical management styles of both Lee Abbey and the Jesus Fellowship are more reminiscent of Christendom than the more egalitarian patterns which the future seems to demand.

In both these and similar situations, pressure has meant that legislation allows for these 'intentional communities' to be recognized as exempt from such things as the statutory minimum wage. This is similar to the exemption given to the historic 'professed communities'.

However, for each success there are costly failures. One needs only to hear of the pain of former members of the Post Green Community, in Dorset, at its break-up, or of the departure of the Fisherfolk and the Community of Celebration from the Isle of Cumbrae in Scotland[10] to recognize this. But following Jesus does mean risk, and that can include crucifying pain as well as resurrection joy.

My task is not to advocate participation in someone else's particular, long-term, residential vision of community. In recent years, due to falling numbers of vocations, the historic professed Order of Prinknash monks have had to move out from their large, modern, purpose-built monastery back into the smaller, more economical, older gatehouse. Not even historic, professed communities are exempt from external pressures. Community carries no guarantee of longevity.

A serious set of options

What I do want to affirm is that those seeking longer-term residential Christian community will find a number of serious options along the post-Christendom spectrum. However, to date, it is almost impossible to offer examples that will surely survive or the patterns which such groups *must* (rather than should) adopt. Joining any community has its risks. It is no surprise that the novitiate for many historic religious communities was seven years. One only needs to watch *The Sound of Music* to realize that not everyone can or does have a vocation to residential, long-term community.

It may be such wise recognition which has led to the growth of 'dispersed community' in recent years. Some, like the Ashram, Grail, Iona and Othona communities, began as denominationally oriented, respectively Methodist, Roman Catholic, Church of Scotland and Anglican. All have now evolved towards wider ecumenical memberships. Others, like the Northumbria Community, were deliberately multi-rooted, drawing leaders and creating supporter groups from Anglican, Baptist and New Church sources.

Simple involvement in any of these dispersed communities' programmes, their literature and daily prayer cycles, their activism, conferences and weekend or week-long retreats, should help prospective members. The key question is to discern how and whether that particular community's nature will empower this individual's daily discipleship. But the next question must be: How will it enrich the person's home church, too?

Increasingly in post-Christendom, as local churches withdraw, tortoise-like, from engagement, some of the dechurched will turn to such dispersed communities to 'be church' for them. However, it behoves the maturity of traditional Christian leadership to let this happen as times and society change.

There will be many like me who sit on the fringe or perhaps at the heart of different discussions towards new forms of post-Christendom dispersed community.

As an example, for some years a number of people from the Anabaptist movement or who are Jesus-centric Quakers have been engaged in conversations (meeting electronically, personally and, less frequently, for overnight and weekends retreats) towards creating a form of community. The Radix Community[11] is envisaged as a small network of communal urban eco-households committed to neighbourhood activism, peace-making and developing urban farming, supported by a wider network of individuals. To date, it has been unsuccessful in raising funds to create households in deprived areas; twice losing properties at the last moment. Now members are offering interest-free £1k loans to enable successful purchase of the next targeted property. Each household will be led by a mature couple, with a number of younger people, working part-time on a 'mustard seed' basis[12] to help fund their living costs, and voluntary activism. To some this will seem like an idealistic pipedream. Another longer-term objective is to work towards building an eco-village. To the Radix Community these are an achievable vision, already working in hearts, prayers, wallets and times together. It may take some years to realize even part more fully.

But what this illustrates is that for some, and they are not alone, there is a recognition that post-Christendom will require many different new responses. So the prayer, vision, discernment and hard work need to begin sooner rather than later. A vision, such as that of the Radix Community just outlined above – but it could be one of several contemporarily evolving visions – is encouraged by other emerging or renewed responses.

The present discussions within the Iona Community to restore their network of Columban houses, initially in Scotland and south-east England, shows that others with track records in community believe the time is right to renew this pattern of communal disci-pleship. The surge of interest in varying forms of Christian community[13] suggests that more individuals and 'pockets' are also being led to consider this direction. This does not mean the death of the local congregation, but merely another strand of develop-ment along the spectrum of shared Christian discipleship.

Eat, pray and . . .

What all, inherited and emerging, Christians can share is relaxed conversation over a meal. My hope is that this volume has given enough encouragement to you to take that risk whether with friend or stranger. 'Offers of food or a meal together are central to almost all biblical stories of hospitality, to most historical discus-sions of hospitality, and to almost every contemporary practice of hospitality . . . Shared meals are central to every community of hospitality – central to sustaining the life of the community and to expressing welcome to strangers.'[14]

My encounters with a number of emerging churches from Glasgow to Glastonbury carry increasing testimony to shared households. Often this can simply be a case of a single person lodging with a couple or family, without any long-term com-munity vision or shared household prayers, except when host-ing the 'emerging church' involved. Sometimes it can be a lot more.

North of Bolton, two couples have bought a Pennine terraced home together, hoping to build an 'emerging church' through their mobile-van-based organic food business. While all secular wisdom may scream against such close ties between couples, faith, home and business, it easily harks back to early church models.

Long before anyone ever mentioned post-Christendom, both David Clark[15] and Andrew Lockley[16] were in the vanguard of UK studies of varying forms of community, including Christian com-munity. Some were activist. Others, like Birmingham's Brandhall Baptist Church, bought or rented houses, setting up communal households, simply to provide church members with living space without the stress of buying or having to rent locally.[17] However, many of the longer-lived shared households and proto-communities prefer to retain anonymity. Given the contemporary economic downturn, shared Christian households may become even more necessary.

Perhaps it is the British mentality that finds intentional community 'somewhat difficult', as a leading URC figure recently told me. Yet from the alternative culture stable, the Diggers and Dreamers directories[18] contain no such prissiness from New Age and other faith communities. We have much to learn from them, as well as groups in North America, the Netherlands, France and Australasia, in developing intentional Christian communities, based within shared households and local congregations. While we Anabaptists frown on pride, it is a joy to me that many of the longer-lasting shared households *and* proto-communities do acknowledge their debt to the Mennonite tradition.[19]

Just as away-days are great opportunities for learning, so too are congregational weekends, which can give people a taste of what Christian community means or even looks like. Utilizing residential centres, such as those operated by the Othona Community, where everyone shares in the manual tasks, bed-making and washing-up, can significantly reduce costs.

Some congregations, like St John's, Haydon Wick, alternate their annual church weekend between a home-based event (like Emmanuel's) and going to a residential conference centre; spreading costs over two years makes this economically viable for almost all. However wonderful such weekend community experiences are, anyone who recalls life in a family or seminary will begin to realize that intentional longer-term community has real pitfalls. These must be engaged with and that may begin, drawing upon the practical experiences of others.[20]

A divorced Catholic acquaintance came to see me, having left a North Wales Ignatian retreat prematurely. When he booked, he realized that the experience of silence was to be nurtured there. He was not prepared for retreat participants to be asked to suppress all opportunities for conversation, even when on country walks. While relishing the opportunity to pray and eat as a group, he regretted the lack of talking together. That centre's advance publicity has greatly improved and now explains the restrictions. Most people need intentional community experiences to eat, pray *and talk*. Very few of us are called to silent households.

Post-What . . .?

Post-Christendom's influence marginalizes the church as wider society's political correctness abounds. Yet as that same political correctness attempts to offend Islam less, Christians may find their sense of persecution increases. At Easter 2011, a housing association care worker was disciplined by his employer for keeping a palm cross stuck to his vehicle's dashboard. Incidents such as this are becoming more frequent. Shock descends upon older residents when clergy are attacked in local neighbourhoods.[21] How long before Christians generally become targets? Many urban church buildings are often targets already. The sharing of homes may become a necessary step if active Christian disciples have to adopt a safety-in-numbers approach.

Even if people do not recognize nor understand the term 'post-Christendom', there needs to be a recognition that British and western European society is changing. Inherited churches and traditionalist leadership need to 'wake up and smell the coffee' – perhaps literally. There does need to be a re-evaluation of how mission is both exercised and prayerfully co-ordinated. To take a maxim from the business world: 'If we fail to plan, we plan to fail.'

Mutually encouraged?

Perhaps if we allow ourselves to be encouraged by 'emerging churches' as well as Jesus' own words and example, even the most traditional of inherited congregations may recognize that change is needed. An increase in both hospitality and community is not alien to our Christian tradition but essentially part of it. So ask yourself: How many folk really do not want to be invited nor have a good meal among peace-loving folks? Simply inviting someone to join us for Sunday lunch moves the concept of 'church' from a building to a table, from a brief hour to a time of real sharing.

We need to be mutually encouraged. We need to recognize the mutual interaction between 'inherited' and 'emerging' patterns, recognizing that both *can* draw on each other's strengths and can learn from each other's weaknesses. Both need to be part of the changes necessary to meet the challenge of post-Christendom. We can do that by becoming 'communities of transformation'. That may begin with just some folks being encouraged to invite others for Sunday lunch or a midweek meal. But as relationships strengthen and friendships grow, a sense of true and biblical community can develop.

'Communities of transformation accept the radical risk of the gospel and go into rather than retreat from the turbulent waters of our times. They go not because they have the answers but because God has called them there . . . Communities of transformation are people committed to the journey of the banquet together.'[22] Learning to enjoy sharing meals together builds a sense of generous and outward hospitality. In turn, as others encounter us in a relaxed way and can move into friendships at their pace, a new sense of relationship occurs. Very naturally we can become communities of transformation.

Conclusion

To complete this book, I offer five basic conclusions:

- Whether it is Cardinal Cormac Murphy O'Connor's remarks, quoted at the head of Chapter 9, *or* the fact that Paternoster as a major UK Christian publisher are onwardly publishing this *After Christendom* series, *or* the arguments of this series' writers or mine in this volume, something called 'post-Christendom' is increasingly recognized. This is marginalizing the Christian church, to the fringes of society, in most people's thinking and the attitudes and world-views of most large spheres of societal influence, such as those of education and the media. That marginalization pushes the Christian community back towards the place in society which it occupied in the first few centuries after Jesus' death and resurrection.
- The Christendom church occupied a privileged position, in power, influence and wealth. It allowed a multi-layered, almost hierarchical pattern of beliefs, enabling a lowest-common-denominator-involvement by the masses. If they paid their tithes, did not deny the Creed and attended worship on 'high days and holy days', many could (sometimes literally) 'get away with murder'. Against this background, many radical movements reacted with more egalitarian forms of Jesus-shaped discipleship, causing them to be oppressed, exiled, and sometimes persecuted and executed. These latter groups necessarily had to forge patterns of hospitality and community far more committedly than Christendom's followers, in order to survive the opprobrium and violence directed towards them.

- Hospitality is at the heart of Jesus' ministry, whether 'welcoming outcasts' or 'eating with tax-gatherers and sinners'. The New Testament Christians 'practised hospitality' and the early church continued that sharing – Acts 2:42–7 offering advocacy and example, suggesting patterns of community. Coenobitic Christian monasticism is widely recognized in the first few centuries AD. The symbiotic practice of hospitality and community occurred within Christendom's historic monasticism and its twentieth-century resurgence in ongoing dispersed communities. These practices speak of patterns of Christian discipleship which continually find acceptance and re-invention.

- It is my conclusion that generating hospitality strengthens relationships, builds friendships and can help to nurture Christian discipleship. As a practice, Jesus is our exemplar and it is biblically advocated. It is not culturally bound and is easily contextualized. Hospitality is an everyday practice, which can be offered to friend and stranger. There is benefit and blessing to both the giver and the recipient. For Christians who know the blessing of the Lord's table, practically and biblically from Psalm 23 to Jesus' 'in memory of me', hospitality is a prophetic activity. Hospitality declares God's kingdom where all are welcome and there will be bread for all.

- It is my contention that the interest in and practice of Christian community is growing. This is now taking place in shared households, dispersed communities with national or regional supporters (who may or may not gather with some kind of frequency and pattern) and longer-term intentional communities, both large and small. All these patterns of groups will gain in importance when the sharp edge of post-Christendom attitude cuts away the support that once Britain's (and Europe's) churches believed was automatic and also their right. Whether or not particular individual groups survive, as ways of cohering discipleship locally, is less important than the potential contribution of 'community'. Hospitable Christian communities of increasingly varied types and numbers will have a growing and increasingly influential place in the spectrum of post-Christian Britain and north-western Europe.

So I encourage you to plan a meal, invite some friends, and discuss the ideas in this book in a relaxed way over food. Then decide how and when you will meet to share hospitality, food and conversation again. Prayerfully decide whether this group can use a table liturgy on this or a subsequent occasion, then even dare to think you might write your own.

Table Liturgies

As Alexander Campbell declared: 'The Church is essentially, intentionally and constitutionally one, whenever it gathers',[1] echoing Jesus' promise to be in the midst of two or three believers who gather in his name. Using these radical and biblical premises, a group meeting as a table fellowship is just as fully a 'church', or assembly of believers, as any Spring Harvest rally or cathedral congregation with all their liturgical 'i's dotted and their theological 't's crossed.

Table liturgies are not always comfortable for folks from a 'non-book culture'. However, their repeated and multi-voiced use can enable newcomers to become comfortable with them but we should always be prepared to adapt the liturgy for our local context.

However, as your group's words become increasingly familiar to its members, memory occurs and people relax into the 'table liturgy', making it an easy vehicle in which to share welcome, a meal, and their personal experience of faith as well as bread and wine.

Equally, eating together is not something which everyone experiences regularly. Folk need to be made welcome and to feel 'at home'. I have shared table liturgies when the main course has been bought-in fish and chips or delivered pizza or take-away curries with supermarket yoghurt (six for £1) as the dessert. However, as a frequent cook, I prefer to serve home-cooked food, usually with home-baked bread or home-grown salads or fruit. Some groups naturally prefer a (planned) bring-and-share meal as a theological statement that we all share from what God has blessed us with. Whatever you do, relax and make it enjoyable.

These liturgies were forged by four different Anabaptist-oriented groups. Their original shape came together because of the work of the Pilgrim group in Charente, France in 2002-3. The brief 'statement of faith' was drawn together during a short group retreat at Glastonbury. The 'Ll?n gathering', Wales, drew together the 'gathering words', some of the biblical responses and the closing prayer. A group of table church co-ordinators met for a day at the London Mennonite Centre to share resources, ideas and a meal. I was blessed to be the note-taker and compiler for all four groups.

There will be those (more likely from the 'inherited churches') who will find 'table churches' and 'table liturgies' less than easy because of either their presuppositions or denominational rules about who can do what if bread and wine are to be shared in this way. There is no intention to offend, but the very nature of post-Christendom thinking will challenge such preconceptions. Do we really believe in a God who listens selectively only to those who have been commissioned in a particular way?

Two table liturgies are reproduced here. Many groups who have devised their own will recognize common elements. You may wish to use these. Copyright does not allow you to photocopy them but you may reproduce them. However, should you wish to produce them, in whole or in part, for resale or in permanent booklet form, copyright must be acknowledged thus: 'Compiled by Andrew Francis for London Mennonite Centre © 2010' and permission sought via www.menno.org.uk

A Table Liturgy for Congregational Use

It is suggested that the congregation sit around a long refectory table, either single or U-shaped; if numbers dictate then the tables can be set in a continuous menorah pattern. This is to facilitate the individual giving of bread and wine to the person next to them – that is excluding the use of stewards or 'sidespersons'.

Leader 1   We come together as the people of God

All   **to eat together in this day which God has blessed us to share.**

Leader 2   We gather in the name of Jesus, our Saviour and
                example

Women   **to speak and to listen as he has taught us to do,**

Men   **to serve one another as he has shown us.**

Leader 3   We open our hearts, minds and lives to receive
                his gifts

All   **to help us be alert to the challenge of this day.**

Pause

Leader 1   We now welcome each other in the name of Jesus
                whose table is spread before us.

*Each person turns to those on their right and left and across the table to
share a hug, a handshake or a word of greeting.*

Leader 2   We have gathered in the name of Jesus

Women   **aware of the provision spread on the table before us,**

Men   **aware that we have come with our past hurts,
                hard words and brokenness.**

All   **Gracious God, send your Spirit afresh upon us
                now**

Women   **that we may know that in this community, you can
                make us whole**

Men   *that here we may experience your love and forgiveness.*

Grace or a prayer of thanksgiving for the meal is said by one person OR a song is sung by all present. The main (course of the) meal is now served. When all have eaten . . .

Reader   Let us listen now to some words and work of Jesus, our Lord, as they are recorded in (name)'s Gospel, chapter (number).

The Gospel is then read.

Reader   This is the word and way of Jesus

All   **whom we choose to follow this and every day.**

Dessert, fruit or cheese and biscuits are served; while this eaten, the gathering discuss together the gospel extract which has just been read. Then after those series of conversations . . .

Leader 3   Let us speak together of the faith we are called to share.

All   **We believe in Jesus, God's word in our humanity**

Women   **who was born of Mary**

Men   **to share our common life, tears and laughter.**

All   **We believe in Jesus**
who welcomed the stranger and healed the sick
who ate with outcasts and sinners
teaching and revealing the way of the kingdom.

We believe in Jesus
who was betrayed, accused and killed,
that we might have life in all its fullness
and share his resurrection life.

Leader 1   In this, we recall the life and example of our Saviour Jesus

Women	**who ate with poor and rich, tax-gatherers and sinners**
Men	**who now calls us to be faithful to the ways of his kingdom.**
Leader 2	We remember the story of the night of his betrayal
All	**when he gathered with his disciples**
Women	**to share the Passover meal**
Men	**and to encourage them to realize what this sharing together means.**
Leader 3	to remind them that his life was to be given up for them.
Women	**So Jesus took bread from the table, blessed it, broke it and gave it to them**
Men	**So Jesus took wine from the table, blessed it and gave it to them.**
All	**Now we do as Jesus has invited us to do as we too have these gifts of bread and wine.**

Pause

Women	**Gracious God, we thank you that you have given bread for our table and bread for the world.**
Men	**We thank you that as we break and share this bread that you send your Spirit upon us**
All	**that we celebrate your kingdom.**

The bread is broken and a large portion is given to the adjacent person, who breaks a small piece off, giving this back to the donor, saying 'the bread of life'; the bread is handed on similarly until all are fed.

Pause

Men: **Gracious God, we thank you that you have given wine for our celebration and wine for the world to herald your banquet.**

Women **We thank you that as we share this wine you send your Spirit upon us**

All **that we celebrate your kingdom.**

The common cup is filled and passed to the adjacent person, who drinks then passes the cup on, saying 'the wine of the kingdom'; the wine is handed on similarly until all have shared from it.

Pause

A song may be sung, or coffee/tea may be served.

Leader 1 We gather to pray for the concerns of the day

All **Lord Jesus, hear our prayers for those who struggle and are in need for those we know – sick in body, mind or spirit and for the tasks and ministry you have set before us.**

There follows a time of silence or for open prayer.

Leader 2 Let us say the prayer which Jesus taught us

All **Our Father . . .**

Leader 3 Let us rededicate ourselves to the work of our lives.

All	As we follow in the way of Jesus today,

All   As we follow in the way of Jesus today,
help us to be more faithful in our discipleship.
At the stove and desk, on the land and
workbench,
teach us to be more welcoming, to share our
bread,
to go the extra mile and turn the other cheek.
For we are God's people with his story to tell
and his gifts and grace enliven our living.

Let us step out afresh into the challenge of God's
world

The grace of the Lord Jesus Christ, the love of
God
and the fellowship of the Holy Spirit
be with us all evermore – Hallelujah!

© *Andrew Francis/The London Mennonite Centre 2010*

A Table Liturgy for Home-Based Use

This version is suggested for a group of up to twelve or fourteen who are seated around a single domestic dining table.

Leader 1   We come together as the people of God

All   **to eat together in this day which God has blessed us to share**

Leader 2   We gather in the name of Jesus, our Saviour and example

Women   **to speak and to listen as he has taught us to do**

Men   **to serve one another as he has shown us.**

Leader 3   We open our hearts, minds and lives to receive his gifts

All   **to help us be alert to the challenge of this day**

Pause

Leader 1   We now welcome each other in the name of Jesus whose table is spread before us.

In turn, the whole group greets each individually, who then personally responds before the next person is greeted; thus:

All   **We welcome (Name) in the name of Jesus**

Person named   Thank you, my sisters and brothers.

When all have been greeted . . .

Leader 2   We have gathered in the name of Jesus

Women   **aware of the provision spread on the table before us**

Men   **aware that we have come with our past hurts, hard words and brokenness.**

All   **Gracious God, send your Spirit afresh upon us now**

Women   **that we may know that in this community, you can make us whole**

Men   **that here we may experience your love and forgiveness.**

Grace or a prayer of thanksgiving for the meal is said by one person OR a song is sung by all present. The main (course of the) meal is now served. When all have eaten . . .

Reader   Let us listen now to some words and work of Jesus, our Lord, as they are recorded in (name)'s Gospel, chapter (number).

The gospel is then read.

Reader   This is the word and way of Jesus

All   **whom we choose to follow this and every day.**

Dessert, fruit or cheese and biscuits are served; while this eaten, the gathering discuss together the gospel extract which has just been read. Then after those series of conversations:

Leader 3   Let us speak together of the faith we are called to share.

All   **We believe in Jesus, God's word in our humanity**

Women   **who was born of Mary**

Men   **to share our common life, tears and laughter.**

All   **We believe in Jesus**
                 who welcomed the stranger and healed the sick
                 who ate with outcasts and sinners
                 teaching and revealing the way of the kingdom.

                 We believe in Jesus
                 who was betrayed, accused and killed,
                 that we might have life in all its fullness
                 and share his resurrection life.

Leader 1   In this, we recall the life and example of our Saviour Jesus

Women   **who ate with poor and rich, tax-gatherers and sinners**

Men   **who now calls us to be faithful to the ways of his kingdom.**

Leader 2   We remember the story of the night of his betrayal

All   when he gathered with his disciples

Women   to share the Passover meal

Men   and to encourage them to realize what this
sharing together means

Leader 3   to remind them that his life was to be given up for
them.

Women   So Jesus took bread from the table, blessed it, broke
it and gave it to them

Men   So Jesus took wine from the table, blessed it and
gave it to them.

All   Now we do as Jesus has invited us to do as we too
have these gifts of bread and wine.

Pause

Women   Gracious God, we thank you that you have given
bread for our table and bread for the world.

Men   We thank you that as we break and share this
bread that you send your Spirit upon us

All   that we celebrate your kingdom.

The bread is broken and a large portion is given to the adjacent person, who breaks a small piece off, giving this back to the donor, saying 'the bread of life'; the bread is handed on similarly until all around this one table are fed.

Pause

Men   Gracious God, we thank you that you
have given wine for our celebration and
wine for the world to herald your
banquet.

Women   **We thank you that as we share this wine you send your Spirit upon us**

All   **that we celebrate your kingdom.**

The common cup is filled and passed to the adjacent person, who drinks then passes the cup on, saying 'the wine of the Kingdom'; the wine is handed on similarly until all have shared from it.

Pause

A song may be sung, or coffee/tea may be served.

Leader 1   We gather to pray for the concerns of the day

All   **Lord Jesus, hear our prayers**
for those who struggle and are in need
for those we know – sick in body, mind or spirit
and for the tasks and ministry you have set
before us.

There follows a time of silence or for open prayer.

Leader 2   Let us say the prayer which Jesus taught us

All   **Our Father . . .**

Leader 3   Let us rededicate ourselves to the work of our lives

All   **As we follow in the way of Jesus today,**
help us to be more faithful in our discipleship.
At the stove and desk, on the land and
workbench,
teach us to be more welcoming, to share our
bread,
to go the extra mile and turn the other cheek.
For we are God's people with his story to tell
and his gifts and grace enliven our living.

Let us step out afresh into the challenge of God's world

The grace of the Lord Jesus Christ, the love of God
and the fellowship of the Holy Spirit
be with us all evermore – Hallelujah!

© *Andrew Francis/The London Mennonite Centre 2010*

Bibliography

In recent years, and after many academic bibliographies too, I have become intrigued by different ways of presenting booklists – think of Shane Claiborne's style of showing a bookshelf of actual covers.

For those who want to follow academic pathways from this volume, the referenced footnotes will enable the relevant volumes to be sourced.

What I am presenting here is an annotated booklist in alphabetical order of title. These 'recipe books' helped me and my friends to explore themes of hospitality and community further. They include both works of theology and cookery books for reasons explained below.

It is often said, 'Food fuels friendships and begins to undo prejudices.' So we need to both literally 'practise hospitality' (Heb. 13:2) and learn to practise it well if we are to build community. 'Good food and delightful meals can remind us of the many ways in which God's grace becomes incarnate in our lives' (Shannon Jung, *Food for Life*, p. 106). Learning to cook, and sharing food with both friend and stranger may become as important as sharing the teaching of learned tomes . . . but we always need to revolve our discipleship around the Jesus of the gospels.

Part of that simplicity is gradually to collect the cookery books we need via charity shops and second-hand internet booksellers. In so helping save the planet, and simplifying our westernized diets, we re-affirm our solidarity with Jesus' global community. Enjoy.

Alpha Cookbook, The
(No named writer)   London: Alpha International, 1998
A great congregational resource with several basic recipes, each
with ingredient listings for different sized groups – every church
building's kitchen or catering team should have one.

Anabaptism: Radical Christianity
Andrew Francis   Bristol: Antioch Papers, 2010
An inexpensive primer about Anabaptism, its history, core prac-
tices and principles.

Barbecue Cookery
Cecilia Norman   London: Panther, 1984
Everyone has their favourite barbecue cookbook; barbecues are a
socially acceptable way of gathering crowds in parks, on beaches
or wherever to engender conversation and laughter.

Believers' Church, The
Donald F. Durnbaugh   Scottdale: Herald Press, 1985
One of (if not) the best introductory primers to the history and
character of radical Protestantism. This should be required
reading for anyone with translocal responsibilities in church
planting.

Best of Mennonite Fellowship Meals, The
Phyllis Pellman Good & Louise Stoltzfus
          Intercourse, PA: Good Books, 1991
900 varied recipes for group cooking, ranging from household-
to congregational-sized recipes and quantities. Some American
measures/food names are a delight to translate, as well as
taste.

Body Politics
John Howard Yoder   Nashville, TN: Discipleship Resources, 1991
Yoder's short, brilliant treatise of five key practices of and for
radical congregations is an essential study resource for all moving from inherited to more radical mindsets and mission policies.

Change of Conversion and the Origin of Christendom, The
Alan Kreider   New York: Trinity Press, 1999
An academic but readable treatment of the title's subject, demonstrating how much of our contemporary malaise was part of the very Christendom system from its inception.

Cheap and Easy
Rose Elliott   London: Fontana, 1988
If we want to be welcoming, we need to note that at least one in eight folk is vegetarian. Meat-eating cooks often forget that, so this is great book to start exploring vegetarian catering. (PS: I'm not vegetarian!)

Christian Community in the 21st Century
John Vincent (ed.)   Sheffield: Ashram Press, 2011
A compendium of 3,000-word essays, each portraying different forms of 'network' and 'dispersed' communities with specific post-Christendom mission objectives in one of their leaders' words.

Church After Christendom
Stuart Murray   Milton Keynes: Paternoster, 2004
The second volume in the *After Christendom* series helpfully sets out an agenda, ideas, possibilities and challenge for the advancing post-Christendom era affecting north western Europe.

Church Comes Home, The
Robert & Julia Banks   Peabody, MA: Hendrickson, 1998 (2nd edn)
An encouraging handbook, full of ideas and quality reflection, about the nature and growth of home-based churches as well as their potential for mission and networking.

Communion Shapes Character
Eleanor Kreider   Scottdale: Herald Press, 1997
A questioning and helpfully authoritative book which provides further background to those wishing to explore Chapter 4, 'Gathering at the Table', further.

Complete Cookery Course
Delia Smith   London: BBC, 1978
Don't mock. If you cannot afford evening classes to learn to cook, this book will teach you all the basic techniques and much more. Good cooking + genuine invitation = hospitality-plus.

Eastern Vegetarian Cooking
Madhur Jaffrey   London: Arrow Books, 1981
Eating less meat is healthy for both you and all God's people on the planet. Combining vegetarian and a simpler eastern diet is inexpensive, helping to challenge our western insularities.

English Bread and Yeast Cookery
Elizabeth David   London: Penguin, 1979
If we believe in 'bread for all', we need to be able to make everything from flatbreads to table-fellowship-sized loaves. This will teach you how . . . and a whole lot more.

Extending the Table: A World Community Cookbook
Joetta Handrich Schlabach   Scottdale: Herald Press,1991
One of my personal favourite cookbooks, reminding me and my guests of how much we owe to others as we celebrate the breadth of God's provision – both in their labours and their lifestyles.

Food for Life: The Theology and Spirituality of Eating
L. Shannon Jung   Minneapolis: Fortress, 2004
A book to help westernized Christians to celebrate and offer hospitality while helping to deal with their guilt at the global inequalities in food distribution.

Good Eating
Stephen Webb   Grand Rapids, MI: Brazos Press, 2001
The author develops a strong 'first modern systematic theology of diet', challenging individual Christians, cells and congregations in their westernized patterns of meat-oriented hospitality.

Living More With Less
Doris Janzen Longacre   Scottdale: Herald Press, 1980
Another significant Mennonite resource primer, challenging
readers towards easier patterns of simpler lifestyle, shared housing, etc. to enable congregations to become localized dispersed
communities.

Making Room: Recovering Hospitality as a Christian Tradition
Christine D. Pohl   Grand Rapids, MI: Eerdmans, 1999
A stimulating overview of Pohl's historical research of hospitality and its imperative, even in north America, for the practice and
purpose of mission as well as the growth of the church.

More-with-less Cookbook
Doris Janzen Longacre   Scottdale: Herald Press, 1976
The archetypal Mennonite domestic cookbook, with great wide-
ranging recipes, sound dietary advice and a radical, but global,
theological perspective. Your home needs this book.

Paul's Idea of Community
Robert Banks   Peabody: Hendrickson, 1994 (rev. edn)
This is Banks' accessible but scholarly treatise on the early House
Churches in their cultural setting. His analysis helps build upon
the New Testament trajectory of the nature of dispersed and
household communities.

Politics of Jesus, The
John Howard Yoder   Grand Rapids, MI: Eerdmans, 1994
The seminal late-20th-century theological and biblical basis for
the radical, Anabaptist-oriented pattern of personal discipleship,
which calls believers away from Christendom's perspectives.

Stations of the Banquet
Cathy C. Campbell   Minnesota: Liturgical Press, 2003
An energizing liturgical resource, rooted in good theology, to
help Christians, individually and corporately, reflect upon
Christian faith's foundations, for our diet, sharing and food jus-
tice.

Taste of Africa, A
Dorinda Hafner   London: Headline, 1994
Like other non-First World cuisines, African food lends itself to easy stretching to accommodate guests in either households or residential communities. Hafner helps to keep a world perspective.

Worship and Mission After Christendom
Alan Kreider and Eleanor Kreider Milton Keynes: Paternoster, 2010
The fifth *After Christendom* volume, which makes clear connections between our patterns of hospitality, liturgical welcomes and the nature of our mission.

Endnotes

1 – Introduction

[1] Martin Jones, *Feast: Why Humans Share Food* (Oxford: OUP, 2007), pp. 207ff.

[2] Michel de Certeau, *The Practice of Everyday Life* (London: UCP, 1988), p. 105.

[3] L. Shannon Jung, *Food for Life* (Minneapolis: Fortress, 2004), p. 19.

[4] Stephen H. Webb, *Good Eating* (Grand Rapids: Brazos Press, 2001), p. 18.

[5] Shannon Jung, *Food*, p. 18.

[6] Jonathan Bartley, *The Subversive Manifesto* (Oxford: BRF, 2003), p. 88.

[7] Christine D. Pohl, *Making Room: Recovering Hospitality as a Christian Tradition* (Grand Rapids: Eerdmans, 1999), p. 6.

2 – What Does the Bible Say?

[1] Anabaptists were part of a radical movement which emerged during the sixteenth-century Reformation. Their role and theology will be more fully explained in Chapter 3.

[2] Or Pentateuch – the Bible's first five books of Genesis, Exodus, Leviticus, Numbers and Deuteronomy.

[3] Craig L. Blomberg, *Contagious Holiness* (Downers Grove: IVP, 2005), p. 33.

[4] Matthew, Mark and Luke – because they share a similar viewpoint. 'Synoptic' comes from the Greek, meaning literally 'with one eye' or figuratively 'with one view'.

[5] Mark 2:15 and parallels; Luke 7:36ff.

⁶ Chapter by Klyne Snodgrass, in *Common Life in the Early Church: Essays Honouring Graydon F. Snyder*, ed. Julian V. Hills (Harrisburg: Trinity Press, 1998), p. 186.

⁷ Bruce Chilton, *Pure Vision: Jesus' Vision of God* (Grand Rapids: Eerdmans, 1996), p. 86.

⁸ Matt. 14:13–21; Mark 6:30–44; Luke 9:11–17; John 6:5–13.

⁹ E.P. Sanders, *Paul and Palestinian Judaism* (London: SCM, 1977), p. 206.

¹⁰ John Koenig, *New Testament Hospitality* (Philadelphia: Fortress Press, 1985), p. 34.

¹¹ Elizabeth Schüssler Fiorenza, *In Memory of Her: A Feminist Theological Reconstruction of Christian Origins* (New York: Crossroad, 1983), p. 142.

¹² N.T. Wright, *Christian Origins and the Question of God*, vol. 2 (Minneapolis: Fortress, 1996), p. 431.

¹³ Chapter by Andreas Lindemann, in *Common Life in the Early Church: Essays Honoring Graydon F. Snyder*, ed. Julian V. Hills (Harrisburg: Trinity Press, 1998), p. 205.

¹⁴ Lindemann, *Common Life*, p. 208.

¹⁵ Blomberg, *Contagious Holiness*, p. 165.

¹⁶ Wayne Meeks, *The First Urban Christians: The Social World of the Apostle Paul* (New Haven: Yale UP, 1983), p. 158.

¹⁷ Robert Banks, *Paul's Idea of Community* (Peabody: Hendrickson, 1994), p. 81.

¹⁸ Koenig, *New Testament Hospitality*, pp. 8ff.

¹⁹ Eschatology is the study of the 'end times'.

²⁰ John R. Donahue, *The Gospel in Parable* (Philadelphia: Fortress, 1988), p. 140–5, quoting Joachim Jeremias, *The Lord's Prayer* (Philadelphia, Fortress Press, 1964).

²¹ Albert Schweitzer, *The Quest for the Historical Jesus* (London: Fontana, 3rd edn, 1951).

²² The Greek word, *parousia*, is also used by writers. In its New Testament context, this refers to the 'Second Coming of Christ' in glory.

²³ Geoffrey Wainwright, *Eucharist and Eschatology* (London: Epworth, 1971), p. 147.

3 – Radical Streams

[1] See the list at the back of the book.
[2] Robert Banks, *Going to Church in the First Century* (Fort Worth, Seedsowers/Christian House Pub., 1990).
[3] Wayne A. Meeks, *The Origin of Christian Morality: The First Two Centuries* (New Haven: Yale UP, 1993), p. 26, emphasis added.
[4] Alan Kreider and Eleanor Kreider, *Worship and Mission After Christendom* (Milton Keynes: Paternoster, 2010), pp. 232ff.
[5] J. Stevenson and W.H.C. Frend, eds, *A New Eusebius* (London: SPCK, 1987), pp. 46ff.
[6] *The Apostolic Tradition of Hippolytus* (Nottingham: Grove Books, 1980).
[7] Roger Collins, *Early Medieval Europe 300–1000* (London: Macmillan, 1991), p. 249.
[8] Andrew Jotischky, *A Hermit's Cookbook* (London: Continuum, 2011), pp. 26ff.
[9] Alan Kreider, *The Change of Conversion and the Origin of Christendom* (New York: Trinity Press International, 1999), pp. 38ff.
[10] Stuart Murray, *Beyond Tithing* (Carlisle: Paternoster, 2000), pp. 153ff.
[11] J.R.H. Moormann, *History of the Church in England* (London: A&C Black, 1953), pp. 68ff.
[12] Bede, *A History of the English Church and People* (London: Penguin, 1977), p. 150.
[13] Trevor Saxby, *Pilgrims of a Common Life* (Scottdale: Herald Press, 1987), p. 86.
[14] Walter Simons, *Cities of Ladies: Beguine Communities in the Medieval Low Countries 1200–1285* (Pittsburgh: Pennsylvania UP, 2003).
[15] René Weis, *The Yellow Cross: The Story of the Last Cathars 1290–1329* (London: Penguin, 2000).
[16] Albert Hyma, *The Brethren of the Common Life* (Grand Rapids: Eerdmans, 1950).
[17] William R. Estep, *The Anabaptist Story* (Scottdale: Herald Press, 1975).
[18] R.M. Stephens, *The Burning Bush* (London: Waldensian Press, 1975).
[19] Brother Ramon SSF, *Franciscan Spirituality* (London: SPCK, 1994).
[20] Andrew Francis, *Anabaptism: Radical Christianity* (Bristol: Antioch Papers, 2010).
[21] David Cornick, *Under God's Good Hand* (London: URC, 1998), p. 64.
[22] Cecil W. Sharman, *George Fox and the Quakers* (London: QHS, 1991).

[23] Donald F. Durnbaugh, *The Believers' Church* (Scottdale: Herald Press, 1985 ed.), pp. 146ff.

[24] Kathryn Spink, *A Universal Heart* (London: SPCK, 1986).

[25] Ron Ferguson, *Chasing the Wild Goose* (Glasgow: Wild Goose, 1998).

[26] Robert Ellsberg and Dorothy Day, *By Little and by Little: The Selected Writings of Dorothy Day* (New York: Alfred A. Knopf, 1983).

[27] Andrew Walker, *Restoring the Kingdom: The Radical Christianity of the House Church Movement* (Sevenoaks: Hodder & Stoughton, 1986).

[28] Simon Cooper and Mike Farrant, *Fire in our Hearts* (Northampton: Jesus Fellowship, 1997).

[29] John Vincent, *Into the City* (London: Epworth Press, 1982).

[30] Nicky Gumbel, *Telling Others* (London: Kingsway, 1997).

[31] Michael Fanstone, *The Sheep that Got Away* (Tunbridge Wells: Monarch, 1993).

[32] Alan Jamieson, *A Churchless Faith: Faith Journeys Beyond the Churches* (London: SPCK, 2002).

[33] Donald E. Meek, *The Quest for Celtic Christianity* (Edinburgh: Handsel Press, 2000).

[34] Allan Armstrong ODP, *Aspects of the Spiritual Life* (Bristol: Antioch Papers, 2010).

[35] Alan Kreider and Stuart Murray, eds, *Coming Home* (Ontario: Pandora Press, 2000).

[36] Stuart Murray, *Changing Mission* (London: CTBI, 2006).

[37] www.urbanexpression.org.uk

[38] www.cruciblecourse.org.uk

[39] www.radixcommunity.org

[40] Christine D. Pohl, *Making Room: Recovering Hospitality as a Christian Tradition* (Grand Rapids, Eerdmans, 1999), p. 42.

[41] John Vincent, ed., *Christian Communities* (Sheffield: Ashram Press, 2011), p. 10.

4 – Gathering At the Table

[1] Stephen H. Webb, *Good Eating* (Grand Rapids: Brazos Press, 2001), p. 141.

[2] From the Greek word *eucharistia* meaning 'thanksgiving'.

[3] Didier Decoin, *Jésus le Dieu qui riait* (Paris: Arthème Fayard, 1999), p. 41.

⁴ Eleanor Kreider, *Communion Shapes Character* (Scottdale: Herald Press, 1997).

⁵ Kreider, *Communion*, p. 223.

⁶ Andrew Francis, *How then Shall We Eat?* (unpublished DMin dissertation, Princeton Theological Seminary, NJ, USA, 2010), p. 18.

⁷ Gillian Feely-Harnik, *The Lord's Table: The Meaning of Food in Early Judaism and Christianity* (Washington: Smithsonian Press, 1994), pp. 71ff.

⁸ Feely-Harnik, *Lord's Table*, pp. 107ff.

⁹ Robert Banks, *Going to Church in the First Century* (Fort Worth: Seedsowers/Christian House Publications, 1990).

¹⁰ Wayne A. Meeks, *The First Urban Christians: The Social World of the Apostle Paul* (New Haven: Yale UP, 1983), pp. 97ff.

¹¹ Robert Banks, *Paul's Idea of Community* (Peabody: Hendrickson, 1994), p. 83.

¹² *The Apostolic Tradition of Hippolytus* (Nottingham: Grove Books, 1980).

¹³ *The Methodist Service Book* (London: Epworth Press, 1975), B14.

¹⁴ *Common Worship* (London: Church House Publishing, 2000), p. 266.

¹⁵ L. Shannon Jung, *Food for Life* (Minneapolis: Fortress, 2004), p. 51.

¹⁶ John Howard Yoder, *Body Politics* (Nashville: Discipleship Resources, 1997), pp. 20–1, italics in original.

¹⁷ Cathy C. Campbell, *Stations of the Banquet* (Minneapolis: Fortress Press, 2003), p. 53.

¹⁸ John Dominic Crossan, *The Historical Jesus: The Life of a Mediterranean Jewish Peasant* (San Francisco: Harper, 1992).

¹⁹ Dale R. Stoffer, ed., *The Lord's Supper: Believers' Church Perspectives* (Scottdale: Herald Press, 1997), pp. 11ff.

5 – Hospitality Creates Community

¹ Christine D. Pohl, *Making Room: Recovering Hospitality as a Christian Tradition* (Grand Rapids: Eerdmans, 1999), p. 150.

² They asked to remain anonymous.

³ Pohl, *Making Room*, p. 71.

⁴ Dale Brown, *Biblical Pacifism* (Elgin: Evangel Publishing, 2003).

⁵ Pohl, *Making Room*, p. 131.

⁶ Stephen H. Webb, *Good Eating* (Grand Rapids: Brazos Press, 2001).

⁷ Alan Kreider and Eleanor Kreider, *Worship and Mission after Christendom* (Milton Keynes: Paternoster, 2010), p. 215.

[8] We return to the imagery of *Babette's Feast* in Chapter 9.

[9] David Bosch, *Transforming Mission* (New York: Orbis, 1996), p. 389.

[10] Kreider and Kreider, *Worship and Mission*, p. 220.

6 – Building the New Community

[1] Sallie MacFague, *Life Abundant* (Minneapolis: Fortress, 2001), p. 175.

[2] Joerg Rieger, *Liberating the Future* (Minneapolis: Fortress, 1998), p. 127.

[3] John Howard Yoder, *The Politics of Jesus* (Grand Rapids: Eerdmans, 1972 edn).

[4] This is a further example of those individuals who are classed as 'dechurched' by researchers; we first encountered this in Chapter 3.

[5] Nils-Arvid Bringéus, *Man, Food and Milieu* (Edinburgh: Tuckwell Press, 2001), p. 34.

[6] Wayne A. Meeks, *The First Urban Christians: The Social World of the Apostle Paul* (New Haven: Yale UP, 1983), p. 77.

[7] Willow Creek is a US church which redeveloped its ministry around a fresh style of Sunday and midweek gathering. Attendees sat around small tables, café-style, while singers and musicians 'performed' and preachers gave soundbite comment pieces, relating that day's news to Bible passages.

[8] Christine D. Pohl, *Making Room: Recovering Hospitality as a Christian Tradition* (Grand Rapids: Eerdmans, 1999), p. 159.

[9] Jean Vanier, *Community and Growth* (London: DLT, 1979), p. 323.

[10] Robert Banks, *The Church Comes Home* (Sutherland, NSW: Albatross, 1986).

[11] Stuart Murray, *Changing Mission: Learning from the Newer Churches* (London: CTBI, 2006), p. 7.

[12] Alan Kreider and Eleanor Kreider, *Worship and Mission After Christendom* (Milton Keynes: Paternoster, 2009), p. 234.

[13] Greenham Common was the site of a 1980s, women-led, peaceful demo against the use of nuclear weapons launched from the UK; the protesters lived in tents and makeshift shelters, next to the perimeter fence of a USAF air-base.

[14] Robert Banks and Julia Banks, *The Church Comes Home* (Peabody: Hendrickson, 2nd edn, 1994).

[15] Banks and Banks, *Church Comes Home*, p. 97.

[16] Banks and Banks, *Church Comes Home*, p. 115.

[17] Dietrich Bonhoeffer, *Life Together* (London: Harper & Row, 1954), p. 27.

[18] Banks and Banks, *Church Comes Home*, p. 188.

7 – What Kind of Community Do People Want?

[1] Lloyd Pieterson, *Reading the Bible After Christendom* (Milton Keynes: Paternoster, 2011), ch. 3.

[2] Andrew Francis, *The Wind of the Spirit* (Sevenoaks: anmchara/HHSC, 2000), p. 14.

[3] W.E. Sangster, *The Craft of the Sermon* (London, Collins, 1954).

[4] Glen Marshall, *Preaching After Christendom* (Milton Keynes: Paternoster, 2014).

[5] Stuart Murray, *Changing Mission* (London: CTBI, 2006), p. 5.

[6] Kathy Galloway, *Living by the Rule* (Glasgow: Wild Goose, 2010).

[7] The concept and nature of the 'mother house' is changing. Those readers familiar with either films such as *The Nun's Story* or *The Sound of Music* or retreats in traditionally ordered monastic houses (or convents) need to shed their preconceptions. There is far more dynamic interaction between the 'wardens' of such motherhouses and their guests; it is a partnership of equals in the equipping of skillsets, exploration of gifts or prayer and in providing space for retreat or learning/teaching.

[8] Arthur Paul Boers, Eleanor Kreider, John Rempel, Mary H. Schertz and Barbara Nelson Gingerich, eds, *Take Our Moments and Our Days* (Scottdale: Herald Press, 2007).

[9] The Northumbria Community, eds, *Celtic Daily Prayer* (London: Marshall Pickering, 1994).

[10] David Clark, *Basic Communities: Towards an Alternative Society* (London, SPCK, 1977), pp. 303ff.

[11] Alan Kreider and Eleanor Kreider, *Worship and Mission After Christendom* (Milton Keynes: Paternoster, 2010), p. 215.

[12] Kreider and Kreider, *Worship and Mission*, p. 220.

[13] E.g. 'Why Have You Forsaken Us?' – a *Sunday Times* magazine analysis (24 April 2011) of the 31 October 2010 siege of Baghdad Cathedral by Islamic extremists, in which 46 Christians died and 70 others were wounded.

[14] Donald B. Kraybill, *The Upside-Down Kingdom* (Scottdale: Herald Press, 1990), p. 149.

[15] Kreider and Kreider, *Worship and Mission*, p. 220.

[16] Pieterson, *Reading the Bible*, p. 141.

[17] Pieterson, *Reading the Bible*, p. 146.

8 – Developing the Necessary Leadership

[1] Robert Banks and Julia Banks, *The Church Comes Home* (Peabody: Hendrickson, 2nd edn, 1994).

[2] As revealed, Genesis, Exodus, Leviticus, Numbers and Deuteronomy; these books are known as the Pentateuch, in the Old or Hebrew Testament.

[3] Walter Brueggemann, *Living Toward a Vision* (New York: United Church Press, 1982), p. 64.

[4] John Howard Yoder, *Body Politics* (Nashville: Discipleship Resources, 1997), p. 47, italics in original.

[5] Robert Banks, *Paul's Idea of Community* (Peabody: Hendrickson, 1994), pp. 144ff.

[6] Stuart Murray, *Church After Christendom* (Milton Keynes: Paternoster, 2004), p. 111.

[7] Yoder, *Body Politics*, p. 54.

[8] Pohl, Christine D., *Making Room: Recovering Hospitality as a Christian Tradition* (Grand Rapids: Eerdmans, 1999), p. 183.

[9] Ian Adams, *Cave – Refectory – Road* (Norwich: Canterbury Press, 2010).

[10] Durnbaugh, *Believers' Church*.

[11] Brueggemann, *Living Toward a Vision*, p. 131.

[12] Abe Bergen, 'Envisioning the Future' in *Congregational Discipling: A Three Fold Vision for Worship, Community, and Mission* (Scottdale: Herald Press, 1997), p. 76.

[13] Murray, *Church After Christendom*, pp. 190ff.

[14] Murray, *Church After Christendom*, p. 191.

[15] Murray, *Church After Christendom*, p. 192, italics in original.

[16] Banks and Banks, *Church Comes Home*, p. 154.

[17] Murray, *Church After Christendom*, p. 192.

[18] Andrew Francis, *The Wind of the Spirit* (Leeds: HHSC/anmchara, 2000), p. 78.

[19] Murray, *Church After Christendom*, p. 193.

[20] Banks and Banks, *Church Comes Home*, p. 45.

[21] Simon Barrow, ed., *Expanding Horizons* (London: Southwark Diocese, 1995), pp. 37ff.

[22] James Schrag, Foreword in *Congregational Discipling* (Scottdale: Herald Press, 1997), p. 9, my italics.

[23] Ken Hawkly, 'Discipling Middle Adults in the Faith Community' in *Congregational Discipling*, p. 118.

[24] Murray, *Church After Christendom*, p. 126.

[25] Brueggemann, *Living Toward a Vision*, p. 11.

9 – Developing the 'Building Blocks'

[1] Quoted in *The Times* and other broadsheet newspapers on 6 September 2001.

[2] John Vincent, *Alternative Church* (Belfast: CJL, 1976).

[3] Dave Cave, *Jesus is Your Best Mate* (Marshalls: London, 1988).

[4] Barbara Glasson, *Mixed Up Blessing* (Peterborough: Inspire 2006).

[5] Joy Mead, *The One Loaf: An Everyday Experience* (Glasgow: Wild Goose, 2004).

[6] Doris Janzen Longacre, *More-with-less Cookbook* (Scottdale: Herald Press,1988), p. 49.

[7] Hymn by Richard Gillard © Scripture in Song.

[8] Christopher Jamison, *Finding Sanctuary: Monastic Steps for Everyday Life* (London: Phoenix, 2007).

[9] Brother Roger, *Parable of Community* (London: Mowbrays, 1980).

[10] Maggie Durran, *The Wind at the Door* (London: Kingsway, 1986).

[11] www.radixcommunity.org

[12] Tom Sine, *The Mustard Seed Conspiracy* (London: MARC Europe, 1984).

[13] John Vincent, ed., *Christian Communies* (Sheffield: Ashram Press, 2011).

[14] Pohl, Christine D., *Making Room: Recovering Hospitality as a Christian Tradition* (Grand Rapids: Eerdmans, 1999), p. 73.

[15] David Clark, *Basic Communities: Towards an Alternative Society* (London, SPCK, 1977).

[16] Andrew Lockley, *Christian Communes* (London: SCM, 1976).

[17] Clark, *Basic Communities*, p. 306.

[18] www.diggersanddreamers.org.uk

[19] David Janzen, *Fire, Salt and Peace: Intentional Christian Communities Alive in North America* (Evanston: Shalom MC, 1996).

[20] Art Gish, *Living in Christian Community* (Sydney: Albatross, 1990).

[21] Christendom reappears when the violence is extreme, such as the nationwide media interest in February 2012 following the murder of the Revd John Suddards, in his Gloucestershire vicarage, where he lived alone.

[22] Cathy C. Campbell, *Stations of the Banquet* (Minneapolis: Fortress Press, 2003), pp. 194–5.

Table Liturgies

[1] Alexander Campbell in his 'Declaration and Address to the Churches of Christ', quoted in 'Stating the Gospel', ed. David M. Thompson (Edinburgh: T&T Clark, 1989), pp. 118ff.

After Christendom Series

Stuart Murray, *Post Christendom*, 978-1-84227-261-9, £9.99
Stuart Murray, *Church after Christendom*, 978-1-84227-292-6, £9.99
Alan & Eleanor Kreider, *Worship and Mission after Christendom*,
   978-1-84227-681-5, £12.99
Lloyd Pietersen, *Reading the Bible after Christendom*,
   978-1-84227-735-5, £10.99
Jo & Nigel Pimlott, *Youth Work after Christendom*,
978-1-84227-605-1, £9.99
Andrew Francis, *Hospitality and Community after Christendom*,
   978-1-84227-747-8, £12.99

Forthcoming

Glen Marshall, *Preaching after Christendom*, 978-1-84227-753-9
Fran Porter, *Women and Men after Christendom*, 978-1-84227-759-1
Jeremy Thomson, *Emotions after Christendom*, 978-1-84227-815-4
   [working title]
Simon Perry, *Atheism after Christendom*
Brian Haymes, *God after Christendom*

Associated titles

Stuart and Sian Murray-Williams, *Multi-Voiced Church*,
   978-1-84227-766-9, £12.99
Stuart Murray, *The Naked Anabaptist*, 978-1-84227-725-6, £8.99